I0802428

For Lori, Zac, Jake, & Josh:

the best team in town, no doubt about it

THE BEST DALLAS–FT. WORTH SPORTS ARGUMENTS

THE 100 MOST CONTROVERSIAL, DEBATABLE QUESTIONS FOR DIE-HARD FANS

JAIME ARON

sourcebooks

Published by Sourcebooks, Inc.
P.O. Box 4410, Naperville, Illinois 60567-4410
(630) 961-3900
Fax: (630) 961-2168
www.sourcebooks.com

Library of Congress Cataloging-in-Publication Data

Aron, Jaime.
The best Dallas-Fort Worth sports arguments : the 100 most controversial, debatable questions for die-hard fans / Jaime Aron.
p. cm.
Includes index.
1. Sports—Texas—Dallas—Miscellanea. 2. Sports—Texas—Fort Worth—Miscellanea. I. Title.

GV584.5.D35A76 2007
796.'097645315—dc22

2007028692

Printed and bound in the United States of America.
POD 10 9 8 7 6 5 4 3 2

CONTENTS

THE MAVERICKS

THE RANGERS

THE STARS

COLLEGES

INTRODUCTION

Like sports? Like Dallas–Fort Worth sports? Have opinions about 'em?

Good. You've come to the right place.

This book features 100 debatable items about all sorts of sports in our area. There will be things you and your fellow sports junkies have argued about before and plenty of new issues sure to spark disagreements.

In a lot of ways, this is sports-talk radio in book form. It's better than tuning in because you control the conversation.

Read a page at a time or a section at a time; it's your call. Skip a part and come back to it or skip it all together; no problem. Just slide in an old ticket stub as a bookmark so you know where you left off. Maybe dog-ear the corner of the pages you like best for handy reference. Feel free to scribble comments in the margin, or even X out sections you think are complete hogwash—after you buy it, that is.

Here are some details on how these 100 items came together.

The questions all come from me. So do the answers. They're based on my experiences and opinions formed while living in Dallas since 1992 and covering sports here full-time since 1999, when I became Texas Sports Editor for The Associated Press.

Of course, they're also tainted by my biases. For the

sake of full disclosure, I grew up in Houston (so I'm anti-DH) and I went to college at Texas in the late 1980s and early 1990s, when the coaching trinity was David McWilliams, Tom Penders, and Cliff Gustafson. (Unlike most Longhorns, I'm more anti-OU than anti-A&M; I only hate the Aggies for four hours the day after Thanksgiving.)

I liked the concept behind this book the minute it was pitched by the publisher. I was really hooked when I brought up question No. 2 (Who should be on a Mount Rushmore of DFW sports?) at an anniversary dinner for my in-laws. The opinions were flying! My sports-challenged sister-in-law even got in on the fun, making an impassioned pitch for Plano product Lance Armstrong. The chatter was fun, especially when counterarguments came packed with strong facts supporting their opinions.

Here's hoping you get into the same heated debates with your family and friends.

Let the games begin!

—Jaime Aron, August 1, 2007

LEADING OFF

IS DFW THE BEST PLACE FOR A SPORTS FAN TO LIVE?

1 Dallas-Fort Worth is certainly the best place to *be* a sports fan. Process of elimination proves it.

Start with the fact we have teams in all four major pro sports: NFL, NBA, MLB, and NHL. Only 12 other metropolitan areas can claim that.

The MLS may not be big-time to many folks, but it still counts as a fifth pro sport. Only five other cities are still in the running now.

Throw in the Arena Football League and our list of contenders is down to Dallas, Chicago, Denver, and New York.

Do any of them have two PGA Tour events every year *and* two annual NASCAR events and an IRL race *and* a horse-racing track good enough to have hosted the Breeder's Cup in 2004?

Didn't think so.

And this being Texas, we also have our fill of rodeo options: the tradition of the Fort Worth Stock Show & Rodeo, the weekly scene in Mesquite, and the denim-and-diamonds crowd at Dallas's annual Texas Stampede.

The biggest thing we're missing is the WNBA, and plenty of people would say we're not missing anything there.

Another knock is that we don't have big-time college sports, even with three Division I-A institutions in the area (SMU, TCU, and UNT) and a fourth (Baylor) not too far away in Waco.

Well, we do have the annual Texas-Oklahoma game at the Cotton Bowl and the annual Cotton Bowl game. Plus, we're an occasional host to the Big 12 football championship game, the Big 12 basketball tournament, and the NCAA basketball tournament. More prime events are likely on the way once Jerry Jones's billion-dollar stadium opens in Arlington in 2009. It already has been picked to host the 2011 Super Bowl.

Another barb might be that this is all quantity, not quality. Well ...

The Cowboys are the most successful team in the nation's most popular sport. They're called "America's Team" for a reason.

The Mavericks have been one of the best NBA teams for several years and should be for several more with Dirk Nowitzki just entering the prime of his career, Avery Johnson calling the shots, and Mark Cuban paying the bills.

The Stars just hosted the All-Star Game and are a playoff perennial. Maybe they don't always last as long as they did from 1998 to 2000, but those postseason runs got folks here hooked on the greatness of playoff hockey.

The Rangers have contributed ballpark nachos and scoreboard dot races to the sporting world, along with some really bad teams. Having won only a single playoff game in 35 years is downright awful, but at least they have a terrific ballpark and provide 81 chances a year to watch big-league baseball. They also have a Double-A team in Frisco, where you can see future big-leaguers from closer up and for less money. Over in Fort Worth we have the independent league Cats, whose games are even cheaper and whose cat's-eye merchandise is among the best-looking in baseball.

Now let's do a little name-dropping: Troy Aikman, Lance Armstrong, Sammy Baugh, "Mean" Joe Greene, Ben Hogan, Lamar Hunt, Jimmy Johnson, Michael Johnson, Tom Landry, Bobby Layne, Bob Lilly, Mickey Mantle, Don Meredith, Mike Modano, Byron Nelson, Davey O'Brien, Johnny Rutherford, Nolan Ryan, Emmitt Smith, Roger Staubach, LaDainian Tomlinson, Lee Trevino, and Doak Walker. All called these parts home at one time or another, and that's only the short list.

Another benefit is having two first-class sports sections in the area—*The Dallas Morning News* and *Fort Worth Star-Telegram*. There also are two established sports-talk radio stations, one on AM and one on FM, each catering to different types of fans.

So while the DFW weather is not as postcard perfect as San Diego, the fans are not as passionate as those in Philly (sometimes a good thing) and there's not as much tradition and history as New York or Boston, the combination of all the things Dallas–Fort Worth *does* have can't be beat.

WHO SHOULD BE ON A MOUNT RUSHMORE OF DFW SPORTS?

2 From the current crop or all time? How about by era? Or a foursome from each sport?

Nope. You only get one chance, just four icons to define the entire area.

With so many ways to go with this, some guidelines need to be established. So we might as well stick with the ones that went into deciding the actual Mount Rushmore.

The idea was conceived in 1923 as a tourist trap first, historical monument second. The faces of George Washington, Thomas Jefferson, Abraham Lincoln, and Theodore Roosevelt were selected because of their broad national appeal, as well as their individual contributions.

Washington was the first great leader. Jefferson helped the nation grow. Lincoln kept the country together in trying times. And Roosevelt represented the modern-day keeper of the flame.

Thus, my 2007 DFW equivalent is:

- Tom Landry
- Roger Staubach
- Nolan Ryan
- Dirk Nowitzki

Here's why:

LANDRY

Years after his death, decades after he left the sideline, Landry's legacy looms the largest of anyone who has ever been part of Dallas–Fort Worth sports.

His stone-faced gaze is so iconic that it's only fitting he be immortalized in rock. The challenge for architects is to put a hat on his head.

For the record, Landry's credentials include being the first coach of the Cowboys and the only coach for the first 29 years, compiling 20 straight winning seasons with 13 division titles, five Super Bowl appearances, and two championships.

He did it all with integrity, too. A pious, principled man, Landry touched the lives of many through his deeds on and off the field, setting a good example for leaders in all professions. His unceremonious dumping by Jerry Jones was awful, except that it generated many heartfelt tributes that showed Landry how beloved he was.

Tex Schramm was a close runner-up for the "Washington" spot because he was as much the patriarch of the local sports scene as Washington was the father of our country. Schramm didn't coin the term "America's Team," but the Cowboys wouldn't have achieved that status without him. Ditto for him making the NFL the powerhouse it is today. Plus, as a promoter at heart, he would've loved a publicity stunt like this.

STAUBACH

Jefferson was a statesman and the drafter of the Declaration of Independence. Staubach was a Heisman Trophy winner from Navy who served his country before giving the Cowboys their independence from the moniker "Next Year's Champions," delivering a Super Bowl title his first year at the helm. Besides, the way the Cowboys dominate the local landscape, they deserve two honorees. One of them has to be a player—and Staubach remains the ideal player. He gets bonus points for being the quarterback of the group that's bringing the Super Bowl to Arlington in 2011.

Sure, Bob Lilly carries the title "Mr. Cowboy" and Troy Aikman has a face that already seems chiseled out of a mountain. But Staubach was the dynamic force who took what Lilly started and turned it into a championship product, building the tradition Aikman carried on.

NOLAN

Landry can't be the only native Texan on our monument. And no one embodies the spirit of the Lone Star State better than Nolan Ryan. Having "Big Tex" on here makes our DFW Rushmore a better place, just like having "Honest Abe" on the real Rushmore.

Although Ryan played longer and had better years in Houston and Anaheim, his time in Arlington was vital to his legacy and to the credibility of the Rangers franchise.

Together, they celebrated his 5,000th strikeout, his 300th

win, and his sixth and seventh no-hitters. He got his face bloodied by a ball off Bo Jackson's bat and kept pitching. He also gave Robin Ventura what he deserved when the punk charged the mound against the old man.

Everything Ryan did sparked interest in the Rangers, which in turn helped get the public funding needed to build The Ballpark in Arlington. An All-Star game came to the new place and soon after the franchise righted itself long enough to win three division titles.

DIRK

Still angry about the Golden State series? Still bitter about what happened against Miami in the NBA Finals?

Get over it. Step back and look at the big picture, the one that includes Nowitzki accepting the NBA MVP trophy a month before his 29th birthday.

Only halfway through his career, he's already the greatest player in franchise history. He's also the best player among all local teams—has been for several years and probably will be for more to come.

Already the leading rebounder and 3-point scorer in team history, Nowitzki is on pace to become the top scorer during the 2007–08 season. And just because he hasn't led the Mavs to a championship yet doesn't mean he can't.

Roosevelt was a controversial choice for Rushmore because history hadn't had long enough to judge his legacy. The decision-makers behind Rushmore were willing to take the risk, and I am, too.

Washington, Jefferson, Lincoln, and Roosevelt did so much to make our country what it is today. Landry, Staubach, Ryan, and Nowitzki have done the same for the DFW sports scene.

WHAT WAS THE BIGGER STUNNER: MAVS-WARRIORS IN MAY 2007 OR THE JIMMY-JERRY DIVORCE IN FEBRUARY 1994?

3

How could a Mavericks team that played so great for so many months bow out of the playoffs so meekly?

How could a team owner get rid of a coach who'd just brought him two straight Super Bowl titles and had the talent in place to win a bunch more?

Nobody can say they saw either one coming. But retrospect does provide some clues—more in the Mavs' case.

Dallas had struggled against Golden State for two years, which includes the year before Don Nelson became coach of the Warriors. One of the Mavs' first mistakes might have been paying too much attention to the extenuating factors surrounding each of their losses.

Another problem was that the Mavericks went into the playoffs on a bit of a lull, having not played meaningful games in about two weeks, while the Warriors were on a 9–1 roll.

Dallas also came in carrying expectations heightened by a record-setting regular season. Everyone knew they had to win it all or the season would be considered a failure. More than that, though, a championship would've made them one of the greatest single-season clubs in NBA history and quite an inspiration: The team that choked in the finals then came back and finished the job.

Whatever players were thinking, their thoughts were scrambled by coach Avery Johnson's decision to shake up the starting lineup in Game 1. That move didn't cost them the series, but it sure set a bad tone.

Over on the Golden State side, everything the Warriors touched turned to, well, gold. Nellie pushed all the right buttons, turning Dirk Nowitzki into a helpless bystander while Baron Davis and Stephen Jackson became the headliners.

Whether the Warriors exposed flaws or pulled off a fluke is another debate. The bottom line is that they won, pulling off what has to be considered the biggest upset in NBA playoff history.

The good news? Something even more bizarre happened to a local team.

At a time when the Cowboys should've been pondering

how many more consecutive Super Bowls they might win, Jerry Jones went around telling folks he wasn't getting enough credit—and that coach Jimmy Johnson was getting too much credit—for the two they'd already won. Jones went so far as to utter his infamous line about any of 500 coaches being able to win with the talent he was paying for.

That did it. Johnson wanted out. And Jones was more than happy to let him go.

The breakup seems as ridiculous now as it did then. In fact, the way things have played out since then is the reason I'm going with the Cowboys' craziness over the Mavericks' meltdown.

Jones dumped Johnson so he could take control. Well, look how things have turned out. Barry Switzer got Dallas to the brink of the Super Bowl the next year and won it all the year after that. Yet since winning one more playoff game in 1996, the Cowboys haven't gotten within sniffing distance of a Super Bowl. They've changed coaches and players plenty of times, but the results, and the general manager, pretty much stay the same.

Would Johnson have won more than one more Super Bowl? Would he have better prepared the team for life after Troy Aikman, Michael Irvin, and Emmitt Smith?

A Jimmy-Jerry personality clash likely was bound to happen sooner or later. But at the time it happened? Even with the benefit of hindsight, that's still more stunning than the fresh wound of the Mavs-Warriors series.

WHAT WAS THE BEST TRADE MADE BY A DFW TEAM?

4 There's a tall German guy acquired in a deal with Milwaukee who's made such a big impact locally that he's on our version of Mount Rushmore.

That would be the slam-dunk pick—if the Cowboys hadn't pulled off one of the most lopsided trades in the history of all pro sports, the Herschel Walker deal.

Let's start by reviewing the arrival of Dirk Nowitzki, because the full story is better than you probably realize.

The Mavericks had been eying Nowitzki for months, having seen him up close when a team of foreign youth stars worked out in Dallas on their way to the Final Four in San Antonio. The Celtics were in on the secret, too, and the Mavericks knew it. Yet getting the big German was still Plan B on the day of the 1998 draft. Dallas's primary target was Steve Nash, then a third-string point guard for the Phoenix Suns.

Mavs' exec Donnie Nelson was riding his motorcycle when the caller ID on his cell phone showed a number from the Phoenix area. He knew it was Suns' boss Danny Ainge saying they had a deal. Part of it, though, required the Mavs to make another deal. The brilliant part is they used the subsequent deal to snag Nowitzki.

Hang with me here because this is where the details get tricky.

The Mavs had the sixth pick, the Celtics the tenth. Dallas knew that the teams picking seventh and eighth were set on taking players other than Nowitzki. So Milwaukee, at No. 9, was the perfect trading partner.

At the request of the Bucks, the Mavericks took Robert "Tractor" Traylor. Two heart-stopping picks later, Nowitzki was still available and Milwaukee snagged him for Dallas. Then Milwaukee used the 19th pick on Pat Garrity and sent him and Nowitzki to the Mavericks for Traylor.

Garrity was the guy Phoenix wanted. Dallas included him in the deal with the Suns for Nash.

Thus, in the same night, through separate-but-connected trades, the Mavericks acquired Nash *and* Nowitzki, the two players who did so much for the revival of their franchise.

Garrity lasted eight seasons in the NBA. Traylor was gone within five years.

Awesome, right?

Yet still not as good as the Walker deal. Let's review the juicy details, which still draw smiles from Cowboys fans and tears from Vikings fans. (Heck, some Redskins, Giants, and Buffalo Bills fans might get emotional about it, too, albeit more along the lines of anger and envy.)

On October 12, 1989—with Jerry Jones and Jimmy Johnson less than nine months into their NFL careers—the

Cowboys sent Walker and four draft picks to the Minnesota Vikings for five players and eight draft picks.

The number of picks involved was crazy from the start. Even crazier:

- Dallas got three first-rounders and three second-rounders.
- The best Minnesota got was two third-rounders.

The Cowboys weren't done dealing. Packaging a pick here and another there, they moved all over the draft board for several years. Emmitt Smith, Darren Woodson, Russell Maryland, and Kevin Smith are among the selections that can be traced to the Walker deal.

The Vikings made the trade because they thought Walker would put them over the top.

Haunted by an 0 for 4 Super Bowl record—remember, this was back before Buffalo lost four straight—Minnesota seemed to be close to a championship. The Vikings had narrowly lost the NFC Championship game following the 1987 season. In 1988, they had the NFL's best defense and one of the top offenses, but didn't make it out of the second round of the playoffs.

So in 1989, with Walker coming off his best season, Minnesota general manager Mike Lynn swallowed hard and gambled. Lynn ended up being right about the deal building a championship team.

Vikings coaches never figured out the best way to use Walker. He was there only three years and didn't run for 1,000 yards in any of them. Minnesota ended up not winning a playoff game until eight years later. By then, the Cowboys had parlayed their stockpile of picks into three Super Bowl titles, and even had Walker back on their roster.

So be sure to smile the next time you hear the names Herschel Walker, Danny Ainge, and Pat Garrity. Save your biggest smile, though, for Mike Lynn.

WHAT HIGHLIGHT INVOLVING A DFW TEAM DO YOU NEVER GET TIRED OF WATCHING?

5 Let's go for a six-pack of clips, running through them countdown style:

6. SEPTEMBER 24, 2000—THE T.O. TAKEDOWN

Safety George Teague "defended the star" with a blindsided hit of 49ers receiver Terrell Owens after his second celebration on the midfield logo at Texas Stadium. Some of the joy has been sapped since Owens joined Jimy Jones's payroll.

5. MAY 26, 1993—JOSE CANSECO'S HEADER

Seeing a fly ball bounce off Canseco's head and go over the fence in Cleveland for a home run is hilarious even if you don't know a thing about sports. Knowing about sports, and knowing about Canseco, makes it even funnier. Befitting the Rangers' history, it happened while he was playing for them.

4. JANUARY 3, 1983—T.D.'S 99-YARD TD

Tony Dorsett's 99-yard touchdown run, the longest in NFL history, is a record that can't be beat. It's made better by the fact that Dallas had only 10 men on the field. No Cowboys appearance on "Monday Night Football" is complete without seeing this romp against the Minnesota Vikings.

3. JUNE 20, 1999—"NO GOAL?" HA!

Brett Hull's Stanley Cup-winning goal against the Buffalo Sabres is even better if you can watch it with someone from Buffalo. Hearing them whine "No goal!" and drone on about Hull's skate being in the crease is still satisfying—and something to think about any time a call goes against a Dallas team in any sport.

2. DECEMBER 28, 1975—THE ORIGINAL "HAIL MARY"

This play is always a treat, and another that's enhanced by watching it in a group, primarily with a Minnesota Vikings fan. When they scream that Drew Pearson pushed off, counter by asking why their 11 men couldn't stop Dorsett on the 99-yard TD.

The clip of the Roger Staubach-to-Pearson answered prayer would probably top this list if someone could dig up the postgame interview with Staubach. See, that was when he used a line about having closed his eyes and said a "Hail Mary," putting that religious term into the football vernacular.

1. AUGUST 4, 1993—ANOTHER KIND OF PUNCH-OUT FOR THE RYAN EXPRESS

Nolan Ryan whipping up on Robin Ventura is a clip that still draws huge cheers every time it's shown at The Ballpark.

Every time I see the 26-year-old Ventura throw down his bat, sling off his helmet, and indignantly charge after 46-year-old Big Tex, I can't help but laugh because I know what's coming. It's the same thrill people get from watching pro wrestling or going to an auto race for the crashes.

Ryan just stands there and puts Ventura in a headlock so easily you'd have thought it was choreographed. Then come the uppercuts: one, two, three quickies. Ryan rears back for No. 4, throws another little one then gets in one last good lick, all with his pitching hand.

Ventura and his manager were tossed. Nolie stayed. Pudge Rodriguez picked off Ventura's pinch-runner and Ryan threw 4-plus more innings without giving up a hit. He was the winning pitcher, too. He won again when the commissioner suspended Ventura for two games, Ryan for none.

Knowing the background makes this one-sided brawl even better.

Ryan was angry with himself for not fighting back when Dave Winfield charged at him in 1980. He vowed never to make that mistake again. From 1981–92, he never got a chance with any of the 74 batters he hit or the dozens more he scared. He had to wait all the way until Ventura was foolish enough to try.

Ventura was the only person Ryan plunked in 1993. Better yet, he wound up being the last hit batter of Ryan's career.

Revenge is sweet, especially when captured on video.

WHAT MOMENT MAKES YOU MOST WANT TO HURL A BRICK AT YOUR TV?

6

There were more candidates for this list than the good-moment list, perhaps because bad moments so often come down to one clear, defining moment.

Still, here's another six-pack of clips. You might need a six-pack of your own to drown some sorrows.

6. JANUARY 6, 2007—TONY ROMO'S FLUB IN SEATTLE

All the Pro Bowl quarterback had to do was take a ball he'd already caught and stand it on its tip. Holding for kicks was the only thing he'd done for the Dallas Cowboys in 2004, '05, and the first six games of '06, so he knew the drill pretty well. He'd never messed it up—until now, preventing Martin Gramatica from kicking a short field goal that would've given the Cowboys their first postseason win in a decade. Romo almost added to his growing legend by running for a first down or maybe even a touchdown, but he was stopped just short in what proved to be the final game of the Bill Parcells era.

But that was only a wild-card game. Not painful enough.

5. JUNE 18, 2006—GAME 5 OF THE NBA FINALS

Lots of plays to choose from, but the one that matters most starts with the Miami Heat's Dwyane Wade running toward midcourt, leaping and catching an inbounds pass as he lands on the other side of the stripe. He dribbles back into the frontcourt, sends Jason Terry tumbling with a forearm shove to the hip, dribbles away from Devin Harris, dances around Josh Howard, and cuts back between Harris and Dirk Nowitzki. He finally goes up for a scoop shot that has no chance of going in—but draws a whistle from the officials because Nowitzki may have grazed Wade with a fingernail.

The play symbolized everything that went wrong for the Mavs in their near-miss of the title: mistakes by Dallas, great plays by Wade, and questionable calls by the Heat's friends wearing black and white. (Or should that be Mark Cuban's *enemies* in black and white?)

Agonizing. Still, not excruciating enough, even when factoring in the timeout charged to Howard *between* free throws.

4. DECEMBER 31, 1967—THE ICE BOWL

The Arctic atmosphere (wind chill of minus 48) is painful to imagine. The stakes were high. And it all came down to one play: Green Bay quarterback Bart Starr sneaking through a hole opened because Jethro Pugh's cleats didn't grip the icy turf, especially not when shoved by Packers guard Jerry Kramer and center Ken Bowman.

But the Cowboys weren't the Cowboys yet. They were still "Next Year's Champions," a label given because they couldn't win the big one. (Like the previous season, when the Cowboys lost to the Packers in another NFL championship game. Don Meredith threw a potential tying touchdown into the end zone, but it was intercepted with 28 seconds left.)

3. JANUARY 17, 1971—O'BRIEN'S CHIP SHOT

In Super Bowl V, Baltimore's Jim O'Brien kicked a 32-yard field goal with five seconds left to shut the door on Dallas again.

Chuck Howley became the only MVP from a losing team, but in reality the Cowboys didn't exactly play championship ball that day. The frustration of it all was best expressed by Bob Lilly hurling his helmet, the distance of his fling—20 yards? 30? 50?—depending on who is telling the story.

2. JANUARY 21, 1979—JACKIE BLEEPING SMITH

Back to the Super Bowl, version XIII.

It's Cowboys vs. Steelers and the good guys are trailing 21–14 late in the 3rd quarter. Roger Staubach finds tight end Jackie Smith *wide freaking open* in the back of the end zone. The pass didn't hit him between the 8 and 1 on his jersey, but it was pretty darn close, especially for the guy who had the most receiving yards by a tight end in NFL history, earning him a spot in the Pro Football Hall of Fame.

Staubach is still quick to defend Smith for this one, noting that Dallas got a field goal on that drive. However, the Cowboys lost 35–31, the 4-point difference having slipped right through Smith's hands.

It's hard to top that. Yet one moment does:

1. JANUARY 10, 1982—"THE CATCH"

Joe Montana's scrambling heave might have been an attempt to throw the ball out of the end zone, until Dwight Clark pulled it down over the reach of Everson Walls. It didn't merely cost the Cowboys a Super Bowl. It turned the tide of the franchise—no, make that two franchises.

Dallas didn't come so close to a championship until Jimmy Johnson and the Triplets (Troy Aikman, Michael Irvin, and Emmitt Smith) rebuilt the franchise a decade later. Danny White's best chance to escape Staubach's shadow ended that day in San Francisco. And the 49ers' championship era was launched.

All in one play.

WHO WILL YOU NEVER FORGIVE FOR DISSING YOUR TEAM?

7 This isn't about hating Bryan Marchment for taking out Joe Nieuwendyk and ruining the Stars' chances of winning it all in 1998, the year before they got to drink from Lord Stanley's Cup.

It's not even being mad at Dwyane Wade for the 2006 NBA Finals.

This is about holding a grudge toward Kiki Vandeweghe for refusing to be part of the first-year Mavericks, even if he later came back to work for the team.

It's about loathing Terrell Owens, no matter how many touchdowns he scores for Dallas, because of all his audacious, anti-Cowboys acts before wearing the star himself.

This is about Randy Johnson toying with the Rangers when he was a free agent in 1999, just to up the bidding. And it's about Roger Clemens pretending to consider the Rangers when he knew all along that if he played in 2006 it would be for the Astros, Yankees, or Red Sox.

This is especially about the Pro Football Hall of Fame voters and their "anti-Cowboys bias." Although they've doused such talk in recent years by electing Rayfield Wright, Troy Aikman, and Michael Irvin (with Emmitt Smith a no-brainer when he comes up), they haven't righted all their wrongs.

Bob Hayes was a pioneer and a heck of a player, yet that wasn't enough. Cliff Harris, Chuck Howley, Lee Roy Jordan, Harvey Martin, and Drew Pearson all deserved more consideration than they received.

Only six players from Tom Landry's heyday have made the Hall. That's simply not enough, not for teams that had 20 straight winning seasons and went to the playoffs 18 times in that span, reaching five Super Bowls and winning two championships. It's especially out of whack when you consider there are more representatives from the 1970s Steelers (four titles) and Raiders (one title), and about the same from the Vikings (0 for 4 in Super Bowls) and Chiefs (0 for 1).

Even more curious is that Harris, Pearson, and Martin were all named to the all-decade team from the 1970s, picked by many of the same people who vote on the Hall of Fame. While there are six other all-1970s picks not in the Hall, the anti-Cowboys notion is fueled by the fact Dallas is the only team with multiple players omitted.

Those actions speak for themselves. But DFW sports history also has its share of folks dissing our teams with words—including two recent examples by some big-time names.

Alex Rodriguez actually did both. His action was getting enriched by the Texas Rangers, then getting traded to the team of his choice, the New York Yankees. His gratitude, and inflammatory choice of words, came when he coauthored a story for *ESPN: The Magazine* in which he described the agony of his final season in Texas like this:

> *I remember driving home with my wife, Cynthia, after a game and telling her, "I just don't see the light. Where is the light? What am I in this for?" I would have never gone to Texas if they had told me, "**Alex, it's going to be you and 24 kids.**" Never. For no amount of money.*

We also have to include Emmitt Smith, who during his first training camp with the Arizona Cardinals looked back on his final season with the Cowboys and told *Sports Illustrated* it was ...

> *...the worst year I ever went through playing football. Too much damn drama. Too much selfishness by too many guys on the team. Too much media frenzy around the team. People always looking to me for answers, and I didn't have the answers for them about why we were so bad. **It felt like being a diamond surrounded by trash**. It was just a mental grind.*

Emmitt has enough goodwill equity that he's forgiven.

As for A-Rod and the rest, why let any of them of them off the hook? That's why there is no winner to this section—just a bunch of losers.

BEST LOCAL TEAM OWNER?

8 First, appreciate that Dallas–Fort Worth has three pretty good team owners: Jerry Jones, Mark Cuban, and Tom Hicks. These guys usually do what they think is right to try to improve their teams.

Still, they're far from perfect, with their biggest mistakes hashed out later in this book.

HICKS

Hicks has two horses in this race, although it's not clear whether that helps or hurts his evaluation. After all, one of them is the Rangers.

The other is the Stars, winners of our area's most recent championship team. Then again, it's worth noting that he just wrote the checks for that team, deferring to general manager Bob Gainey and club president Jim Lites in a sport he was still learning.

It's hard to blame him for the hockey team's struggles since then. The biggest knock could be that he's stuck by GM Doug Armstrong and coach Dave Tippett for too long. While they haven't been as good as predecessors Gainey and Ken Hitchcock, they haven't been terrible, either. Nothing wrong with sticking with good people as long as you still have faith in them.

But good relationships might be Hicks's weakness. Just look at what his friendships have produced in Arlington.

John Hart was a disaster. Buck Showalter wasn't worth the trouble he caused. Scott Boras was the arm-twister behind the signings of Alex Rodriguez and Chan Ho Park, plus the return of Kenny Rogers. And the jury is still out on Jon Daniels.

The longer it takes for either team to meet expectations, the lower Hicks plummets in this ranking.

JERRY

Jones has won the most championships in this group with three, but his most recent was more than a decade ago. Since then, the Stars have won one, the Mavs made it to the NBA Finals, and the Rangers...well, they're the Rangers.

You can't argue with Jones's dedication or his desire to win another title. You can argue with his method—relying on himself to call the shots instead of spending his time and money finding the right people to make the best football decisions.

CUBAN

No, he hasn't won a championship, despite coming oh-so-close in 2006 then breaking hearts in 2007. But the Mavericks are built to be a prime contender for years to come. They're certainly the best team in the area these days and their games are the most entertaining—and not simply because the home team usually wins.

When Cuban took over, the club was lousy. He made people pay attention with his wild antics and he made players around the league at least consider coming to Dallas with all the over-the-top perks he offered.

One thing he doesn't get enough credit for is having kept the team's management intact when he arrived. He could've swept out the old—maybe even should've, considering their track record—and brought in people who would've been indebted to him. Instead, the front office has gone from Don and Donnie Nelson to Donnie Nelson and Avery Johnson. Yes, the end with Nellie was a bit messy, but there's something to be said about such stability at the top. Cuban's not a meddler when it comes to most basketball decisions. He knows that's not his specialty, and that he has good basketball people whom he pays to make those decisions. His involvement in roster moves is strictly financial, although that line gets blurred in the case of Steve Nash.

Cuban is passionate and he's involved. Too passionate and too involved some would say, all the way down to telling the game-day staff which replays to show and when to turn the music up or down. There's no way of knowing for sure whether that works against the Mavs when it comes to officials or decisions made by the NBA office. Yet his in-your-face approach stirs up the notion that it's possible, and that's bad enough. Bottom line: Cuban isn't perfect, but he's the best we've got based on how much the good outweighs the bad.

Don't believe it? Just ask fans of the Pittsburgh Penguins,

Chicago Cubs, and other teams that are up for sale—or, worse, fans who *wish* their favorite teams were for sale. They are the ones filling Cuban's inbox with emails begging for him to take over.

WHOSE START SIZZLED MORE: COACH AVERY JOHNSON OR TONY ROMO?

9 The key word is "start."

For Romo, that's his first six games, when he went 5–1. For Avery, let's end it December 31, 2006, when he won his 100th game in 131 tries—four games faster than the previous best set by Red Auerbach.

Picking such a high point might seem like stuffing the ballot box. Nope. Because the choice is Romo.

There are two reasons, the first being that his success was such a surprise.

Here's a guy who was hardly recruited out of high school, went to a Division I-AA college and wasn't taken in the NFL draft. He didn't throw a pass his first three seasons in Dallas, making his only contribution as a holder. Even then Bill Parcells didn't trust Romo enough to let him throw a pass on a fake field goal.

Romo obviously did something right to keep making the roster. Yet for all the talk about Parcells thinking the kid had the right tools, no one really knew.

He certainly didn't look like much in his first heated action. Having replaced Drew Bledsoe at halftime of a Monday night game against the New York Giants, Romo's first pass was intercepted and returned for a touchdown. The 5-point deficit he inherited turned into a 14-point loss.

Romo made his first start the following Sunday. Things weren't looking good when Dallas trailed by 14 in the 1st quarter, at Carolina. Yet he never panicked. The Cowboys ended up winning by a landslide and setting a nifty team record: most 4th-quarter points, 25.

Dallas lost the next game in Washington, but it wasn't Romo's fault. He threw what would've been a game-breaking touchdown to Terrell Owens, but T.O. dropped it. The Redskins only won because of a wacky ending capped by Washington kicking a field goal after time expired.

Romo's breakout came over the next three games. He was named the NFC player of the week after two of them. The exception? Merely handing eventual Super Bowl champion Indianapolis its first loss of the season after a 9–0 start.

Romo attacked his first Thanksgiving start like it was an all-you-can-eat feast, throwing 5 touchdown passes before the 3rd quarter even ended. A week later, he rallied the Cowboys for a road win over the Giants, giving Dallas a two-game division lead in December.

Things didn't pan out after that. Still, to this point, how much more of a WOW factor could you have?

Well, there is something—the No. 2 reason in picking Romo over Avery: The fact there is nothing better in all of pro sports than succeeding as the starting quarterback of the Dallas Cowboys.

Romo enjoyed every bit of his newfound fame with an aw-shucks attitude while his dimpled grin went from sports pages to gossip rags. There was talk of a link to pop star Jessica Simpson. Then country singer Carrie Underwood showed up with him on the field before the Thanksgiving game. That same afternoon, some fans hung his name in the Ring of Honor. Cowboys owner and Ring of Honor czar Jerry Jones was angry about that—that is, angry at the security guards who took the letters down! That's how giddy everyone was over Romo.

Johnson's rise is pretty inspiring, too.

"The Little General" was the starting point guard—"a coach on the floor," as they say—for the Spurs when they won it all in 1999. In fact, as his playing career was winding down, league general managers voted him the active player most likely to become a coach. Twice. Then he was smart enough to sign up to be Don Nelson's successor in Dallas, instead of going to some lowly team.

The opposite of Nellie in personality and core coaching principle (that's a fancy way of saying he stresses defense instead of offense), Johnson won over the locker room so quickly that Nelson stepped aside far sooner than planned.

Avery knew better than to try turning Dirk Nowitzki into Bill Russell. But the Cajun got the German to buy into his system, which went a long way toward making it succeed.

And succeed it did. Just a quick list of highlights because they are so darn impressive:

- Went 16–2 after replacing Nellie at the end of the 2004–05 season, winning coach of the month honors in April, his first full month on the job.
- In his first full season, Dallas tied a franchise record with 60 wins. The Mavs were the only team among the top 10 in points scored *and* fewest points allowed, a tribute to how his emphasis on defense wasn't hurting the offense too much. He was rewarded with the NBA Coach of the Year award, and Dallas went to the NBA Finals for the first time.
- In his second full season, Dallas broke the franchise record with 67 wins, matching the sixth best in league history. The Mavs won their second division title, had their longest-ever winning streak (17 games), and became the first team with three winning streaks of at least a dozen games in one season. Yes, they followed with one of the biggest upset losses in NBA playoff history—but let's save the gnashing of teeth over that for another section.

Taken as a whole, what Johnson did was impressive and inspiring.

Just not more than RomoMania.

IF YOU COULD HAVE BEEN AT ANY GAME EVER PLAYED HERE, WHICH WOULD IT BE?

10 Note the word "here" because it narrows the field to home games. That means you have to throw out Super Bowls and the Stars' 1999 Stanley Cup clincher. Only games played in Dallas or Tarrant County qualify.

Some Cowboys contenders include Clint Longley's Thanksgiving Day performance against the Redskins in 1974 and, for historical significance, Emmitt Smith running past Walter Payton to become the NFL's career rushing king in 2002. But those aren't all-timers.

Nolan's two no-hitters are great candidates, as are Kenny Rogers's perfect game and the 1994 All-Star game. The debut of David Clyde—the high-school-to-pros phenom in 1973—also jumps out.

The Stars have been here the fewest years, but they've provided the most recent championship. They also gave us several years of playoff thrills before and after their lone championship. In fact, Game 6 of the 1999 Western

Conference finals between the Stars and Colorado Avalanche was the loudest event I've ever attended, and one of the most electrifying.

The '86 NBA All-Star game in Dallas was fine, but the events the night before were more memorable: Spud Webb, a little guy and a Dallas native, beating teammate Dominique "The Human Highlight Film" Wilkins to win the Slam Dunk Contest and Larry Bird winning the first 3-Point Shootout, after going into the locker room and asking everyone else who was going to finish second.

A few months later, the Final Four came to town featuring Dale Brown and 11th-seeded LSU (the lowest ever at that point), Larry Brown and Kansas (two years before the Jayhawks won it all), Mike Krzyzewski getting Duke to the finals for the first time, and Pervis Ellison leading Denny Crum and Louisville to its second title in seven years.

The January 1, 1979, Cotton Bowl in which Joe Montana started building his legend by overcoming cold weather, the flu, and a 22-point, 4th-quarter deficit against the Houston Cougars with a touchdown pass as time expired sounds like a good candidate—until you realize that being at that game would've meant sitting in that cold weather. And plenty of locals still hold a grudge against Montana for "The Catch."

Speaking of the Cotton Bowl, it sure would've been fun to have seen Tommy Lewis come off the Alabama sideline and tackle Rice's Dicky Maegle in 1954. Or, go even further back, and imagine being at a Highland Park High School game in the 1940s, when the backfield featured Doak Walker and Bobby Layne. High school football also provided the unforgettable Plano East-John Tyler game in 1994 that drew national attention, as much for the on-field wackiness (John Tyler blowing a 41–17 lead in the last three minutes, then winning on a kickoff return) as for the homespun announcers using lines like, "Good gosh almighty Joe Friday," and, "God bless those kids, I'm going to throw up."

The pick here, though, is one of the few games to earn a nickname: "Moody Madness."

Just being the fifth and final game of the Mavericks' first-ever playoff series automatically makes it special. The fact that Dallas won makes it even better. But there are so many other layers that make it rise above each and every other game played around here.

Start with the setting: Moody Coliseum, which holds 8,000 fewer people than Reunion and wasn't exactly ready for an NBA game. That's why Keith Grant, a future front-office boss who broke in as the team's equipment manager, spent the night before on his hands and knees taping down a 3-point line.

Why the venue change? A tennis match at Reunion Arena. Building officials scheduled it months before, figuring the fourth-year Mavericks wouldn't need the place on April 26, 1984.

The Sonics were only a few years removed from winning

a championship. They'd also dominated the Mavericks all season. But the teams split the first four games of this series. We pick up the action in the final minute of Game 5.

Seattle has a 6-point lead with 46 seconds left, but Dallas rallies. Rolando Blackman puts up a jumper that hits the front of the rim, somehow spins to the backboard then drops in for the tie. The Sonics have two chances to win in the closing seconds, but miss both shots.

Overtime.

The Mavs are ahead by three points with five seconds left when Jay Vincent goes to the line. He's made 31 straight free throws and needs just one to ice the game and the series.

Clank. Clank. But it's still a three-point lead. What can happen?

After a Seattle basket trims Dallas's lead to one point, there's only one second left and the Mavericks have the ball. Vincent tries killing the clock by bouncing the inbounds pass off Seattle's Tom Chambers, but Chambers catches the ball and hurls a shot that misses by a mile.

Game over. Celebration begins.

But wait! The clock still shows 0:01.

Over the next 14 minutes, long enough that some Mavericks players undress and start showering, the refs decide there was an inadvertent whistle. They call for a do-over. Inexplicably, they give Seattle the ball.

The Sonics' last try is futile. Celebration begins. Again.

Only 9,007 fans were actually there. Don't you wish you could have made it 9,008?

THE COWBOYS

ARE THE COWBOYS REALLY "AMERICA'S TEAM"?

11 Absolutely. When they're winning, that is.

When the Cowboys are down, they are just another team. But when they are up, they are way above everyone else.

Look at the TV ratings from the 2006 season, when the expected combustion between Terrell Owens and Bill Parcells fueled hype early on and the rise of Tony Romo provided more drama later. The Cowboys had the most-watched regular-season games on all of the NFL's television partners: Fox, NBC, CBS, ESPN, and the NFL Network. Their playoff game against Seattle was the No. 1 prime-time program of the week, even though it was on a Saturday night.

Look at the 2007 schedule. Dallas got seven nationally televised games—plus another for a *preseason* game against the reigning Super Bowl champion Indianapolis Colts. The Cowboys opened in prime time against one New York team and got the other on Thanksgiving.

Now go back to their last Super Bowl, in January 1996. It was the No. 2 draw in TV history, behind only the final episode of *M*A*S*H*. That makes it the country's most-watched sporting event. Ever.

OK, there's one caveat here: All those people watching aren't necessarily rooting *for* the Cowboys. Plenty tune in to root *against* them. So? Sports is all about inciting passion. Hatred can be a passion, too. It's apathy that kills teams.

The nickname goes back nearly 20 more years. An NFL Films producer named Bob Ryan was putting together the team's 1978 highlight film and noticed how much support the Cowboys had wherever they played. He figured they were on par with the Celtics, Yankees, and Notre Dame when it came to having a national following. They also sold the most merchandise. So Ryan titled the annual wrap-up video "America's Team."

Tex Schramm knew a marketing winner when he heard it, so he took full advantage of the phrase. So has Jerry Jones, of course. It certainly helped that the clubs led by Troy Aikman, Michael Irvin, and Emmitt Smith were able to carry on the tradition. Dallas's success in the 1990s cemented ownership of the nickname.

Teams in all sports try borrowing the phrase. For instance, a 2005 DVD about the Brooklyn Dodgers was titled "The Original America's Team." It's even happened in the NFL. Just last season, in 2006, the New Orleans Saints were dubbed "America's Team" because it seemed the whole country was rooting for them to get to the Super Bowl a year after Hurricane Katrina ruined their hometown and their home field. As soon as they lost, though, they went back to being merely the Saints.

The Cowboys will never be merely the Cowboys.

WHO SHOULD BE IN THE RING OF HONOR BUT ISN'T?

12

First, some ground rules:

- We have to consider the pre-1989 and post-1989 candidates separately. The year Jerry Jones took over is the dividing line in team history and folks from the two eras should be judged against their contemporaries.
- Remember that Jerry is the judge and jury on the actual Ring of Honor. So the argument of who *should* be next into the Ring of Honor and who *will* be next are different things. It especially changes the discussion about Jimmy Johnson. For our discussion about all these candidates, we're going with *should*.

PRE-'89ers

The Tom Landry era already has produced a dozen Ring of Honor selections, plus the Man in the Hat and his boss, Tex Schramm, who came up with the concept. Too many more might water things down. Still, a few more deserve it, and it should be done soon before all the Jerry-era guys start filling up the spaces.

Let's start with a nonplayer, simply, the guy who started it all: Clint Murchison Jr., the team's founder and owner for the first 24 seasons.

Murchison was remarkably hands-off. He once explained why, calling his relationship with Landry a "professional standoff." See, the boss coached a sixth-grade team that was undefeated. So he proudly noted that he didn't take advice from Landry, nor would he offer any. He did, however, offer Landry a 10-year contract after the 1963 season to show his commitment to the coach when others were railing against him for lousy teams the first few seasons. Not only did Murchison put the right people in place with Schramm and Landry, he was smart enough to keep them there. He also was smart enough to move the team from Dallas to Irving, making Texas Stadium a state-of-the-art facility in its time. Murchison's name belongs on the wall so people will ask, "Who was that guy?"

Drew Pearson is the most worthy among those waiting in the wings. The "Hail Mary" wasn't the only clutch catch he made, just the most famous. This No. 88 was as much the go-to receiver for Roger Staubach as another 88, Michael Irvin, was for Troy Aikman. Pearson led the club in receiving four straight years, covering half of Staubach's tenure. When Pearson retired in 1983, he was the team's career leader in catches and yards.

Harvey Martin is another guy who was a big part of

some great teams. A Dallas native, he led the team in sacks in 7 of his 11 seasons. He holds the club record for most sacks by a rookie, in a season and for a career. His 23 sacks in 1977 are one-half more than the official league record, which dates only to 1982. A four-time Pro Bowl pick, he was the co-MVP of a Super Bowl, along with Randy White, a Hall of Famer and Ring of Honor member.

Now comes the tough part—setting the boundary between really good and great. Seems to me that if it takes too much debate, then the player doesn't deserve it. The Ring has to remain exclusive to be meaningful.

That said, you could still make a good case for Charlie Waters and Ed "Too Tall" Jones. Some who are worthy of being listed among "others receiving votes" include six-time Pro Bowl offensive lineman John Niland, linebackers Bob Breunig and D.D. Lewis, cornerback Everson Walls, and fan favorite Bill Bates. (The pro-Bates argument: "Hey, Brad Davis got his jersey retired by the Mavs!")

POST-'89ers

Putting the Triplets in together was perfect. It had to be done that way. It just shouldn't have been done until all the pre-89ers were honored.

Then again, maybe Jones wanted to get a head start because he knew how many of the guys he turned into millionaires he plans to honor.

Larry Allen is only a question of when. Ditto for Darren

Woodson, as nice of a guy as he was a ferocious hitter. Daryl Johnston belongs, too. The guy literally put his neck on the line for his teammates. Just ask Emmitt Smith and Troy Aikman how much of their success they attribute to the selflessness of the "Mooooose."

Now it gets tricky. We're closing in on the "if it takes too much debate, they don't deserve it" line. That means "others receiving votes" status for Jay Novacek, Leon Lett, Nate Newton, Erik Williams, and Mark Stepnoski.

However, three guys are left straddling the fence: Deion Sanders, Charles Haley, and Jimmy Johnson.

Haley was a key player on three title teams and widely considered the final piece of the puzzle. His most sacks came during the season the Cowboys fell a game short of the Super Bowl. Considering Woodson is the only defender up there so far (on my list), Haley could belong—but only after Woody and many others, especially the pre-'89ers.

Deion was an exciting player and the icing on the 1995 Super Bowl champion cake. But he was mostly a pay-for-play mercenary. While most pro athletes are, he made sure everyone knew how much enjoyed playing that role.

Deion got his money and his ring. Keep him out of the Ring, though.

Finally, the Jimmy debate.

Besides the fact Jerry has the final say, Jimmy's campaign is hurt by him being with the team only five years.

But what a five years!

Jimmy Johnson won two Super Bowls and stockpiled talent both on the field and on his coaching staff. In 1990, he had five future head coaches as assistants and another in the starting lineup. (OK, trivia buffs, they are Dave Wannstedt, Norv Turner, Butch Davis, Dave Campo, Dave Shula, and Jack Del Rio.) When the Cowboys won another title two years after he left, 19 of the 22 starters were guys acquired when Johnson was the coach.

Jerry erred by dumping Jimmy. Putting him in the Ring of Honor won't change that, of course. But it would avoid another mistake.

WHO WAS THE MOST IMPORTANT "TRIPLET"?

13

Troy was the leader. Michael was the heart and soul. Emmitt was the workhorse.

What made them great was how perfectly they clicked, on and off the field. Each recognized how much better the team would be if the other succeeded. Such willingness to share is rarely found in players of their caliber. But, for argument's sake, one has to be placed higher than the rest.

Congrats, Emmitt.

His arrival sparked it all, and not as part of some grand plan. He was the 17th guy taken in the 1990 draft, chosen as somewhat of a consolation prize after another player Jimmy Johnson had his eye on was gone. The Cowboys knew they needed a running back, but it wasn't like they went into the draft saying, "Gee, if we can only get Emmitt Smith, then we'll win a bunch of championships."

That is how it turned out, though.

It usually does with great offenses. Just ask John Elway, who didn't win a Super Bowl until Terrell Davis lined up behind him. Or Dan Marino, who never had a top running back and never won a Super Bowl.

Look at Super Bowl history. The St. Louis Rams and their "Greatest Show on Turf" are the only offensive-oriented team to win it all without a workhorse running back, although Marshall Faulk did plenty of work as a receiver out of the backfield.

Emmitt forced defenses to commit an extra man to the run. That opened things up for the passing game, leading to great reads and great throws by Troy, with Michael serving as either target or decoy. You should also remember that Emmitt was a heck of a blocker, occasionally flipping over an unblocked blitzer.

Yes, a terrific offensive line was part of the reason for Emmitt's success. Well, those guys also kept rushers off Troy, which in turn helped Michael, so that's a wash.

The notion that Barry Sanders or any other running back could've done what Emmitt did—because of the line, because of Troy and Michael—is moot, too. Sanders and others weren't here; Emmitt was.

We're also not talking about Emmitt's place in the pantheon of great running backs. (See Argument No. 30 for more on that.) The Triplets weren't a threesome until the final guy got there. He turned out to be the most important one.

WHAT WAS TOM LANDRY'S BEST TEAM?

14 We've got 29 candidates, 20 of them winning seasons. Twelve of his clubs played for the conference championship and five advanced to the Super Bowl.

Only two of them won it all—the 1971 and 1977 squads—so that narrows things down the easy way.

Time for a closer look at each.

1971

The team was coming off the disappointment of a last-second loss in the Super Bowl, another painful near-miss added to the Cowboys' long list. Widely known as the NFL's bridesmaid, their burden-filled bouquet never felt heavier.

A loss on Halloween left them 4–3. Coach Tom Landry took the drastic measure of benching quarterback Craig Morton and making Roger Staubach the main man.

They didn't lose again.

Dallas led the league in scoring, averaging nearly 4.5 points per game more than the second-best team, and the defense also finished in the top 10. With an 11–3 record, the Cowboys tied Minnesota for the most wins in the entire NFL, but the rules of the day left those teams meeting in the first round of the playoffs. Playing in Minnesota, the Cowboys still won 20–12.

The original "Doomsday Defense" gave up only 6 points the rest of the way—a field goal in the NFC Championship game and another field goal in the Super Bowl. That's it. No touchdowns. And it's worth noting that the Super Bowl loser, Miami, went on to win the next two Super Bowls, with their undefeated season coming the following year.

Dallas's 24–3 victory over the Dolphins exorcised all sorts of demons for the franchise. Landry was carried off the field wearing "the biggest smile you ever saw on his face," as Staubach described it at Landry's memorial service.

This team's lineup sure stands the test of time. Of the 22 Super Bowl starters, half can be found in the Pro Football Hall of Fame or the Ring of Honor.

- **Hall of Fame (7):** Bob Lilly, Roger Staubach, Mel Renfro, Rayfield Wright, Lance Alworth, Mike Ditka, and Herb Adderley.
- **Ring of Honor (4 others):** Bob Hayes, Chuck Howley, Lee Roy Jordan, Cliff Harris, plus Hall of Famers Lilly, Staubach, Renfro, and Wright.

Alworth, Ditka, and Adderley got into Canton based mostly on what they did for other teams. But they were still pretty good if they started in the Super Bowl; Alworth and Ditka even scored touchdowns that day.

1977

With only Staubach, Cliff Harris, and Jethro Pugh still starting from the 1971 team, this was virtually a new club. Most had Super Bowl experience, though, having lost a heartbreaker to Pittsburgh two years before (with yet another to follow the next year).

Like the quarterback change of 1971, this season also was marked by a bold move. Dallas traded its top pick and three second-rounders to Seattle for the right to the No. 2 overall choice, spending it on Tony Dorsett.

He was just part of an amazing set of offensive weapons: Staubach in his prime, Drew Pearson, Preston Pearson, Billy Joe DuPree, Ron Springs, Robert Newhouse, and Tony Hill, then a seldom-used rookie. The defense dominated, too.

In fact, the '77 Cowboys allowed the fewest yards in the league on defense. They also gained the most yards on offense. Only one other Super Bowl champion has pulled off that double feat—the Miami Dolphins in 1972, the year they went undefeated.

This Landry team started 8–0, still the best in club history 30 years later. After a pair of losses, they won their final seven games, counting the playoffs. Dallas capped it by crushing

Denver and its "Orange Crush" defense 27–10 in the Super Bowl. The losing quarterback, by the way, was their old pal Morton.

With the victory, the Cowboys joined the Packers, Dolphins, and Steelers as two-time Super Bowl champs. Landry joined Vince Lombardi, Don Shula, and Chuck Noll as two-time champion coaches.

AND THE WINNER IS ...

Landry called his '85 team his favorite because they were overachievers. The '71 club has to be up there, too, because they were his first Super Bowl champions.

But the '77 club was his best.

By the way, a panel of experts selected by the NFL Network ranked the 1977 team as 11th-best among the first 40 Super Bowl champions. Their mistake was not putting the '71 team in the top 20, too.

WHAT WAS JIMMY JOHNSON'S BEST TEAM?

15 We know the 1989 team that went 1–15 was his worst. And his next two teams were just starting to put things together.

So it really only comes down to 1992 and '93.

1992

Charles Haley arrived and a pretty good defense turned great, with Dave Wannstedt coordinating it for one last year before going to coach the Chicago Bears.

The offense, in its second year under Norv Turner, went from really good to superb. Troy Aikman had his best season (statistically) and Emmitt Smith set club records for rushing yards and rushing touchdowns. Michael Irvin averaged 17.9 yards per catch, the best of his career. Only three years removed from the '89 washout, they were driven to cap their amazing rise with a title.

Dallas went 13–3 in the regular season, then blew past Philadelphia in its playoff opener. Then the Cowboys won the NFC Championship game in San Francisco, beating a 49ers club that had gone 14–2. You probably remember Johnson's postgame declaration in the locker room: "HOW

'BOUT THEM COWBOYS!"

The Super Bowl was more like a coronation, one big party announcing that this club had arrived and that it was going to be the team to beat for years to come.

Dallas whipped Buffalo 52–17. It would've been worse—the most lopsided ever—if Leon Lett hadn't celebrated a fumble return for a touchdown a bit too soon, letting Don Beebe knock the ball away just before Lett crossed the goal line.

If there ever was a "statement" game, this was it. The Cowboys were back, and looked like they planned to be on top for years to come.

1993

There were only a handful of personnel changes from '92.

- Darren Woodson took over at safety.
- Lett overtook Russell Maryland as a starting defensive tackle.
- Dixon Edwards replaced Vinson Smith at linebacker.
- Kevin Gogan replaced John Gesek at right guard. Then center Mark Stepnoski got hurt late in the season and Gesek wound up back in the starting lineup in the Super Bowl.

The biggest difference was the motivation.

The burden of being defending champions hit home from the start. Emmitt Smith wanted to be paid like a two-time rushing champion and Jerry Jones was in no hurry. So Emmitt missed the first two games—and Dallas lost them both.

Everyone remembers Thanksgiving because of another Lett gaffe—sliding across the icy turf and into a spinning ball, bringing alive what would've been a dead ball and letting the Miami Dolphins kick a game-winning field goal.

Those losses left Dallas tied with the New York Giants for the best record in the NFC going into the finale, a head-to-head matchup between the clubs. Smith willed the Cowboys to victory in overtime despite a separated shoulder in what became the signature performance of his brilliant career.

A few weeks later, Johnson kept everyone from getting complacent by calling into Randy Galloway's radio show a few days before the NFC Championship game and declaring, "You can put it in three-inch headlines. We will win the ballgame!" They did, too, despite Troy Aikman getting a concussion that forced him to miss most of the second half.

The Super Bowl wasn't a blowout. In fact, the Cowboys were very vulnerable that night. But the Bills weren't able to take advantage.

AND THE WINNER IS ...

If we're talking head-to-head showdown, both teams playing their best, I'll go with '93. They went 15–2 in games Emmitt Smith played and one of those losses was a Lett-induced fluke. They didn't dominate in the playoffs, but part of it was because of Smith's shoulder injury from the finale.

However, if this was a mythical game with both teams picking up where they left off at season's end, it's 1992 all the way.

WHICH WAS BETTER: LANDRY'S BEST OR JIMMY'S BEST?

16 This one is not as tough as it seems: The Hair beats The Hat, the Port Arthur native topping the man from Mission.

The core of Jimmy Johnson's best club won three Super Bowls in four years and might have had even more if he had been able to keep coaching them. That's consistency. Longevity. Greatness.

Landry himself had that, too. But his best teams—well, it goes back to that whole "bridesmaid" thing again.

They also went to three Super Bowls in four years. However, they lost two of them. Sure, they lost to the Pittsburgh Steelers in their Iron Curtain heyday, and there's no shame in that. Just like there's no shame in finishing behind the Triplets in this race.

It sure would be fun, though, to see them go at it in a computer simulation. Imagine Charles Haley trying to get around Rayfield Wright on his way to Roger Staubach. Picture Michael Irvin trying to get away from Mel Renfro, and Lee Roy Jordan waiting for Jay Novacek to come across the middle. And what about Bob Lilly—could he get past all those Pro Bowl linemen and find his way to Troy Aikman? How would Mr. Cowboy fare in trying to tackle Emmitt Smith?

Now *that's* fantasy football.

DALLAS VS. NEW ENGLAND: WHAT'S THE MOST IMPRESSIVE SUPER BOWL STREAK?

17 Dallas won three Super Bowls in four years (1992–95) and New England won three Super Bowls in four years (2001–04). Which streak was better?

After the Cowboys went 3 for 4, NFL observers said it would never happen again. Not in the salary cap era. So kudos to the Patriots for bucking the odds. But that doesn't make their run better.

Here's the bottom line: What happened in the year both teams *didn't* win it all?

- Dallas: Went 12–4, and then lost in the NFC Championship game. The Cowboys were 10 points from returning to the Super Bowl to seek an unprecedented third straight title.

- New England: Went 9–7 and failed to make the playoffs. The Patriots had to win their season finale just to have a winning record.

The Cowboys were able to keep their depth chart intact, with 13 players starting all three Super Bowls. Only eight starters changed from the 1993 to '95 title teams, and several new starters were backups in 1993.

The Patriots didn't have that luxury. Players came and went, but coach Bill Belichick managed to keep plugging holes and winning games. What New England did in the salary cap era is phenomenal. Yet that doesn't make it more impressive than what Dallas did.

Remember, the Cowboys weren't the only team playing without a cap. And it wasn't like Jerry Jones just went around signing up all the best players. Dallas's roster was built the old-fashioned way, through the draft, trades, and claiming guys basically off the street.

The NFL began its Plan B free agency system in 1989, but it's not like the Cowboys used that to fill holes. Only two starters on the 1992 club who started the run were acquired as Plan B guys: Jay Novacek and Vinson Smith.

Plan B dissolved and full-fledged free agency began the off-season prior to the 1993 season. Yet as the Cowboys put together their run of championships, only three starters came from the free-agent market: offensive linemen Derek Kennard and Ray Donaldson, and Deion Sanders.

OK, Deion was a biggie. But along the way, free agency hurt the Cowboys as much or more, with seven Super Bowl starters and plenty of key reserves leaving to cash in elsewhere.

Plus, there's one more area to highlight.

New England's reign was overseen by Belichick's steady hand and ever-present hoodie. Dallas went from Jimmy Johnson to Barry Switzer. Winning despite the coach isn't easy. But the Cowboys did it—and barely missed the one year they didn't.

MOST HEART-POUNDING VICTORY: CLINT LONGLEY ON THANKSGIVING OR EMMITT SMITH WITH ONE ARM?

18 These were two of the greatest regular-season victories, one with an unknown player leaving a long-lasting memory, the other a career-defining performance by a superstar.

NOVEMBER 28, 1974

Roger Staubach was having a rocky Thanksgiving Day outing against the Washington Redskins. Then he was knocked out about five minutes into the 3rd quarter.

With the Cowboys losing 16–3, coach Tom Landry had little choice but to send in a rookie from Abilene Christian who already answered to the nickname "Mad Bomber."

Clint Longley hadn't played since the preseason. Now Dallas was 6–5 and fighting for a playoff berth. The dreaded Redskins were 8–3 and two weeks removed from a home victory over the Cowboys.

Longley made things interesting with a 35-yard touchdown pass to Billy Joe DuPree. Then Longley marched Dallas 70 yards in 10 plays, with Walt Garrison running in for a touchdown that put the Cowboys ahead later in the 3rd quarter.

The Redskins went back in front 23–17 early in the 4th. A short, lead-padding field goal attempt was blocked by the long arms of Ed "Too Tall" Jones, but the Cowboys weren't able to do anything on their next series.

Washington had a chance to run out the clock, but couldn't. So Dallas got the ball back with 1:45 left and no timeouts.

Longley kept a rally going by getting exactly 6 yards on a 4th-and-6 pass to Bob Hayes, putting the Cowboys at midfield. On 1st down, he threw incomplete to Pearson, who'd dropped a touchdown pass that would've tied Dallas's loss at Washington a few weeks earlier. On 2nd down, he hit Pearson with a perfectly thrown bomb into the end zone. Pearson held onto this one for the tie and the extra point put the Cowboys up 24–23 with 28 seconds left.

Washington's last drive ended with Jethro Pugh forcing Redskins quarterback Billy Kilmer to fumble. Harvey Martin recovered it.

The Cowboys had a lot to be thankful for on this holiday, including their playoff hopes still being alive. They won the next game, too, but lost the finale and missed the postseason for the first time in nine years.

During training camp in 1976, Longley and Staubach got

into a pair of fights. Longley was traded after the second one. He may have only contributed 2 quarters to Cowboys lore, but, oh, what a half it was.

JANUARY 2, 1994

The Cowboys opened the 1993 season trying to defend their Super Bowl title without Emmitt Smith because of a contract dispute. Two losses later, things were settled.

Those losses loomed large when the Cowboys went into the final game on the road against the New York Giants. Both teams were 11–4. The winner got the NFC East title, home-field advantage in the playoffs, and a first-round bye. The loser got a wild-card game the next week.

Dallas went up 10–0 on a short touchdown catch by Smith. On the next drive, he ripped off a 46-yard run, getting dragged down from behind. He landed on his right shoulder—and didn't get up for awhile. Another field goal made it 13–0. An X-ray showed Smith had a Grade 1 separation, the lowest degree.

If he kept playing, he risked making it worse. So? He wasn't coming out.

Smith took a painkiller and slipped a thigh pad under his shoulder pads for extra cushioning. He told the offensive linemen to make sure someone picked him up off the turf after every play. Troy Aikman helped by lowering handoffs and passes. Smith's backup, Lincoln Coleman, tried taking his place. Smith wouldn't let him. With No. 22 on the field, coaches couldn't resist riding him. Smith got the ball on 8 of 16 snaps over the 3rd and 4th quarters, even though his right arm was dangling. All that work wasn't enough, either, as the Giants forced overtime by kicking a field goal with 14 seconds left.

New York won the coin toss, but didn't score. Dallas's turn. On an 11-play drive, 9 went to Smith—6 runs, 3catches. On his final carry, Smith lifted his aching shoulder and stiff-armed Lawrence Taylor, setting up the game-winning field goal.

Smith finished with 229 total yards and a touchdown. His 32 carries and 10 receptions were the heaviest workload in team history. He spent that night in a hospital, an IV and painkillers pumping into his arm.

Had the Cowboys lost, they probably would've had to play the next week without Smith. Instead, he returned in time to help Dallas win another Super Bowl and was named the game's MVP. He also was named MVP of the regular season and was the league's rushing leader, despite having missed those two games.

Because of the higher stakes, Smith's performance tops Longley's—by a heartbeat.

TOUGHEST LOSS: THE ICE BOWL OR THE NFC TITLE GAME IN JANUARY 1995?

19

No matter how much agony that January 1995 game caused—for the Triplets, for Jerry Jones, and for ending Dallas's chance of becoming the first to win three straight Super Bowls—nothing could be worse than *losing* a game played with a temperature at kickoff of around minus 13.

Especially when that game would've sent you to Super Bowl II.

Especially after you'd lost the game that would've gotten you into Super Bowl I in the final minute at home to the same team.

Especially since it wouldn't be until Super Bowl VI that you'd finally get over the hump and win a championship.

And did I mention that it was cold?

Cold enough for the fancy $80,000 heating system under the turf to conk out, turning the famed "frozen tundra" into more skating rink than football field. Cold enough for metal whistles to freeze to officials' lips. Cold enough for announcer Frank Gifford to tell a national television audience that he was going to "take another bite of my coffee." Cold enough for the halftime show to be canceled because the instruments were frozen.

The Cowboys were coming off a 52–14 stomping of the Cleveland Browns in Dallas. Now, on the final day of 1967, they were getting a chance for revenge against Vince Lombardi's boys for a New Year's Day loss in Dallas.

The Cowboys turned a 14–0 deficit into a 17–14 lead. Then Bart Starr began a long, slow drive that nearly reached the end zone. Dallas made a couple of stops, then the Packers called timeout with 16 seconds to go. Starr's unforgettable quarterback sneak followed, giving Green Bay a victory that made the Cowboys' frostbite hurt even more.

Compared to that, what happened at Candlestick Park on January 15, 1995, doesn't seem so terrible.

In their first year under coach Barry Switzer, the two-time reigning Super Bowl champions went 12–4 and then blew past Green Bay for a third straight NFC title game against San Francisco. The 49ers had gone 13–3, so it was played in the muck at their place, Candlestick Park.

Three turnovers in the first five minutes left the Cowboys trailing 21–0. They outscored the 49ers 28–17 the rest of the way, but it wasn't enough.

Dallas made a game of it despite 2 more turnovers, a missed field goal, and some strange play-calling. For instance, who thought it was a good idea to leave Larry Brown one-on-one against Jerry Rice in a pivotal situation?

The play that always sticks out—to Cowboys players and fans—is the non-call on Deion Sanders for a hip check to Michael Irvin when a touchdown would've gotten Dallas within a field goal with five minutes left. Instead, Switzer got a 15-yard penalty for hip checking an official and the game was lost.

Troy Aikman, Michael Irvin, and Emmitt Smith all call it the biggest regret of their career, the one that got away.

It probably was. They just won't get any sympathy from the '67 team.

N-n-n-n-n-n-n-none.

WHAT WAS BETTER: THE ORIGINAL "HAIL MARY" OR DORSETT'S 99-YARD TD RUN?

20 Of all the games played from the start of the NFL through January 3, 1983, the longest touchdown run was a 97-yarder way back in 1939. Then Dorsett went 99, setting a record that could only be tied but not broken, doing so on the national stage of a Monday night game.

Throw in the added degree of difficulty of Dallas not having enough men on the field and you've got a play that's still not as tremendous as the "Hail Mary."

The phrase "Hail Mary" gets used plenty every football weekend, from announcers to fans in the stands to even coaches and players at all levels of football. Yet there's still only one play known as *the* Hail Mary: Roger Staubach-to-Drew Pearson for 50 yards, a touchdown, and an improbable victory.

The young, plucky Cowboys knocked off the big, bad Minnesota Vikings 17–14 on December 28, 1975. The guys came away so confident that they steamrolled the Los Angeles Rams in the NFC Championship game a week later to become the first wild-card team to make the Super Bowl.

The play itself was pretty wild, too.

Pearson had been double-covered all day, held without a catch until this final drive. Then, on a 4th-and-17, Staubach threw a sideline pass that Pearson caught for a 25-yard gain. He actually landed out of bounds, but officials decided that a hit by cornerback Nate Wright prevented him from landing in bounds. First down, Dallas, at midfield.

An incompletion on 1st down stopped the clock with 32 seconds left. In the huddle, Staubach basically told Pearson to go deep. So Pearson took off down the right sideline, with Wright following him stride for stride. Staubach got safety Paul Krause to peel off by faking to the left side. Pearson tried faking Wright, but the cornerback didn't fall for it.

Staubach's heave was underthrown. Pearson had to shift gears to track it down. Wright also adjusted. There was contact, which to this day anyone in purple will insist was Pearson pushing off. The pass ended up going through Pearson's hands at the 5-yard line but somehow got pinned to his hip, secured by his elbow. Wright fell and Krause got there too late to help. Pearson already was in the end zone.

It became known as the "Hail Mary" because that's what Staubach, a good Catholic boy, said he prayed after throwing the pass. Funny thing is, the term now refers to a deep pass thrown into the zone as time expires when everyone knows it's coming. The original happened with a half-minute to go and one-on-one coverage.

So, yes, the Hail Mary was better than the 99-yard run—and all other plays in team history.

IF YOU COULD'VE BEEN AT ANY GAME IN TEAM HISTORY, WHICH WOULD IT HAVE BEEN?

21 Going into the 2007 season, the Cowboys had won 401 regular-season games. They'd played 55 playoff games, eight of them Super Bowls. And they'd won five of those.

Dallas's first Super Bowl, in January 1972, would've been a blast because Tom Landry's guys dominated, leading to a postgame celebration that was filled with relief and joy. But it wasn't a great game. The first Super Bowl for the Triplets, in January 1993, was a big ol' party from start to finish. But, again, not a competitive game. The 35–31 loss to Pittsburgh in the January 1979 Super Bowl was plenty exciting, but it's wrong to pick a loss.

So how about these thrillers, in chronologic order:

- The 1972 NFC Championship game, in which Roger Staubach, in relief of Craig Morton, overcame a 12-point deficit with 2 touchdowns in the final 1:30, followed by Charlie Waters intercepting a pass to keep alive defense of Dallas's first Super Bowl title with a 30–28 win at San Francisco.

- Clint Longley's 1974 Thanksgiving surprise against the Redskins. Staubach's backup was forced into his first regular season game with Dallas trailing its division rival by 13. The "Mad Bomber" threw 2 touchdown passes, including a 50-yarder to Drew Pearson in the final minute, and then the defense held on for a 24–23 victory.
- The "Hail Mary" playoff game in 1975, when a Cowboys team not expected to make the postseason knocked off what many consider the best Vikings team ever en route to a surprise Super Bowl berth. Dallas outplayed Minnesota for most of the game, but trailed until the final drive, when Staubach and Pearson connected for 25 yards on 4th-and-17, and then a 50-yard bomb with 24 seconds left.
- The January 1993 NFC Championship game won 30–20 at Candlestick Park against a loaded San Francisco 49ers team, avenging "The Catch," getting the Cowboys back to the Super Bowl and launching the string of three titles in four years.
- Emmitt Smith's agonizing one-armed performance and an overtime victory at Giants Stadium in the 1993 finale.
- Troy Aikman's 5-touchdown game against Washington, the last a 76-yarder to Rocket Ismail in overtime to win a bizarre 1999 season opener. The Cowboys tied a club record by wiping out a 21-point deficit—all in the final 11 minutes of regulation—with the help of an onside

kick and a blown field goal by the Redskins at the end of regulation.

- The first victory of Bill Parcells's tenure, a Monday night miracle in 2003 that was won in overtime at Giants Stadium and started a 5-game winning streak. Dallas went from leading by 15 points in the 4th quarter to trailing by 3 with 14 seconds left, yet managed to force overtime and then win it, both on field goals by Billy Cundiff, who hit an NFL record-tying 7 in the game.

But there's one more that stands above the rest.

December 16, 1979. The Cowboys, Redskins, and Eagles were in a three-way tie for first place in the NFC East, with Washington coming to Texas Stadium to play Dallas in the season finale.

Dallas had been to three of the last four Super Bowls, but had to win to guarantee a spot in the playoffs. If not, it could have been the last home game for Staubach, who was considering retiring.

The Cowboys fell behind 17–0 early in the 2nd quarter, then Staubach led two long scoring drives—the first capped by rookie Ron Springs, the featured running back in this game because Tony Dorsett was out with an injury; the second coming on a diving touchdown catch by Preston Pearson with nine seconds left in the half. Another TD in the 3rd quarter put Dallas up 21–17.

After Joe Theismann barely overthrew an open receiver for what would've been a go-ahead touchdown, Washington settled for a field goal that made it 21–20. Then an interception led to a TD run by John Riggins and Washington was back in front.

The Redskins stretched the lead to 34–21 on a 66-yard run by Riggins that proved to be the longest of his Hall of Fame career. Washington got the ball back with about five minutes left and fans started leaving.

Charlie Waters, working in the radio booth because an injury kept him off the field, told listeners, "You've got to believe!"

Riggins fumbled, only to have a teammate recover it. The Redskins weren't so lucky when Clarence Harmon coughed it up soon after. Randy White got it for Dallas and, three plays later, Staubach threw a 26-yard touchdown pass to Springs.

Now the Cowboys were within six points with 2:20 to go, but the Redskins could've run out the clock. They didn't because of a dropped pass and Larry Cole throwing Riggins for a loss one play after the big running back gained 8 yards. Washington had to punt.

Starting on his 25-yard line with 1:46 left and no timeouts, Staubach hit Tony Hill for 20 yards, then Preston Pearson for gains of 22 and 25. Just that fast, the Cowboys were on the 8-yard line!

The Redskins blitzed on the next play and Staubach threw a lob to Hill before the defense could get in the way. Touchdown, and a 35–34 Dallas lead with 39 seconds left—

time enough for more drama.

A pass interference penalty gave Washington the ball at the 49 with nine seconds left. The Redskins got to the Dallas 42, but time ran out before Mark Moseley could try a game-winning field goal.

With two TD passes in the final 2:20, Staubach pulled off his 21st fourth-quarter comeback victory and his 14th in the last 2 minutes. His 336 yards passing for the game were the second-best of his career, giving him a club-record 3,586 yards for the season. His 3 TD throws this game gave him 27 for the year, another club record.

The win secured a fourth straight division title for the Cowboys and kept Washington from going to the playoffs. Harvey Martin celebrated by taking a funeral wreath that had been delivered to the Dallas locker room before the game—with the inscription, "From the Redskins"—and tossing it into the visitors' dressing room.

This game had it all: high stakes, drama on the field and off, an intense rivalry, and the benefit of being at home.

It also turned out to be Staubach's last victory, a final unforgettable performance in a career filled with them.

WHO IS THE COWBOYS' BIGGEST RIVAL?

22

"Hail to the Redskins!"

Washington's fight song is the perfect place to start because that was among the first punches in the feud between the franchises.

That's right: Before Jerry Jones wanted to punk Little Danny Snyder, before Steve Spurrier promised Snyder a victory over the Cowboys on the day he was hired, before Tom Landry wanted to avoid being surrounded by Redskins in a TV commercial, before Harvey Martin hurled a funeral wreath labeled "From the Redskins" into their locker room at Texas Stadium, before Clint Longley skinned 'em on Thanksgiving, before Washington coach George Allen enlisted spies, there was Cowboys founder Clint Murchison Jr. buying the rights to the Redskins theme song as leverage in his battle with Washington's owner, George Preston Marshall.

Marshall reneged on a deal that would've let Murchison buy the Redskins, and then he tried blocking Murchison's attempt to get an expansion team. Murchison earned Marshall's support only after he bought the rights to "Hail to the Redskins" from another person Marshall had wronged.

So, they made a swap. Murchison gave up the song;

Marshall gave up blocking Murchison from getting his team.

Voilã—a rivalry was born. Washington got its only win in 1960 against Dallas, figured there'd be plenty more, and arranged for them to become division rivals. The teams have met twice a year almost every year since. The only exceptions: a third meeting in the 1972 NFC Championship game and an unusual pair in 1982—a single regular-season game because of the strike, and then a second meeting in the NFC Championship game. (The Redskins won both NFC title matchups.)

Going into the 2007 season, Dallas led the all-time series 55–37–2. The Cowboys had beaten the Redskins more than any other team; they also had their second most losses against them.

But as much as the Redskins provide an annual grudge match, there's another side to the concept of a rivalry that's worth considering. It's the question of what team you take the most satisfaction in beating.

This isn't about kicking a team while they're down, which has happened at times in the Dallas-Washington series. This is about wanting to beat a particular team when they are at their best—especially when you are also at your best, two top dogs fighting for one prize.

And for Dallas, that has to be the San Francisco 49ers.

The Cowboys and 49ers have met in six NFC Championship games: 1970, '71, '81, '92, '93, and '94. Dallas won four, going on to win the Super Bowl after three of them. San Francisco won two, going on to win the Super Bowl both times. Of course, that includes "The Catch" by Dwight Clark in the 1981 game.

So on any given Sunday, the chant should be, "Down with the Redskins!" But on Sundays in January, when the games are the most meaningful, the chant should be, "Bring on the Niners...and stomp 'em!"

JERRY JONES: PRO OR CON?

23 He fired Tom Landry. And Jimmy Johnson. Worse, he hired Barry Switzer, Chan Gailey, and Dave Campo. The trade for Joey Galloway was foolish. Drafting David LaFleur on Troy Aikman's recommendation was silly. Heck, most of the drafts were pretty bad when Larry Lacewell was whispering into his ears.

Sorry, folks. Gotta take the bad with the good. And Jones provides more good than bad.

Start with the three championships the Cowboys have won since Jones entered the league in 1989. No team has won more in that span; only New England has won as many.

You can argue all you want about him being along for the ride, saying Jimmy Johnson assembled the talent, Norv Turner put in the winning offensive system, and the

Triplets executed it. All true—but they still happened on Jerry's watch.

You can't deny his commitment. The guy pretty much sold everything he had to buy the Cowboys and dedicated himself to making sure it worked. It was far from a sure thing.

He stepped on toes at first because he didn't know protocol or chose to ignore it. Remember his previous job: oil wildcatter. High risk, high reward. That's how he runs his NFL team, too. You'd have to say he's hit more gushers than dry holes, especially when you add in all the money he's made for the league, from marketing innovations to negotiating TV contracts.

Jones is as driven now as he was the day he started, and it's only partly because he has a $1 billion, 100,000-seat stadium to fill with fans in 2009. He's still trying to prove he can win a Super Bowl without Johnson or any connection to him. Even he knows the title won by Barry Switzer had Jimmy's fingerprints all over it.

Here's a quote from Jerry the day Wade Phillips was hired. He was talking about his motivation to win another Super Bowl after the one in 1995. Read into it as you wish:

> *I had made a deal that if He would give me one more, I wouldn't ask for another one. Now I've been spending a long time trying to figure out a trade to ask for another one.*

What fans should appreciate the most is that Jones has kept the Cowboys relevant. He always does and says things that give you something to talk about, whether it's through a hiring or firing or by throwing around his money.

Jones knows all this makes him an easy target for criticism. Think he cares? Love him or loathe him, you have to admire his thick skin (insert your own face-lift joke here).

The often-used line is that Jones is a good owner and a bad general manager. But it can't really be separated like that. It's all or none, pro or con.

Pro.

TEX SCHRAMM MADE SOME WILD DRAFT PICKS: WHICH WAS HIS BEST?

24 Getting the "fastest man in the world" in the seventh round is good. Getting a Heisman Trophy winner who would go on to make the Hall of Fame in the 10th round of the same draft is even better.

The best, though, is an easy choice.

If you haven't already guessed, here are some clues:

Heisman Trophy winner; had two tours of duty with the club; made his biggest contribution by leaving!

Herschel Walker was a fifth-round pick, the 114th player taken overall, in the 1985 draft. For the record, it was a pick acquired from Houston for Butch Johnson—pretty fitting considering all the draft picks the Cowboys would get by trading Walker.

Walker was in a long-term deal with Donald Trump's New Jersey Generals of the USFL when Schramm rolled the dice. Walker got out of that deal in August 1986 and joined the Cowboys soon after. What he did for the Cowboys hardly matters, even if he was really good at times. His place in team lore is secure because of the trade with the Vikings. But Dallas never would've had his rights had Schramm not gambled on him in the draft.

Schramm's picks of Bob Hayes and Roger Staubach in 1964 showed his knack for mining gold from the late rounds. He tried striking again in 1967 with a basketball player out of Kentucky who never even played college football. Schramm envisioned Pat Riley becoming a pretty good wide receiver. In 1984, Schramm went the Hayes route again—sort of—by taking another Olympic champion: Carl Lewis.

One of Schramm's final fliers paid off years after he'd left the club. With the second-to-last pick in his last draft in charge, Schramm gambled that Chad Hennings—the Outland Trophy winner—might still be interested in playing football after he got out of the Air Force.

An 11th round pick in 1988, Hennings spent some of the next four years flying missions in Iraq, then joined the Cowboys in '92. The 27-year-old rookie was part of the defensive line rotation that won Super Bowls in three of his first four years.

Schramm wasn't with the Cowboys by then, but you can be sure he took pride in having drafted Hennings—and Walker, since that move proved to be his gift that kept on giving.

JERRY JONES HAS MADE SOME WILD FREE-AGENT SIGNINGS: WHICH WAS HIS WORST?

25

Jones has made some boneheaded moves over the years:

BRYANT WESTBROOK

He was given $1 million to help fix a problem at cornerback. Coaches lost faith in him after just one game—albeit a brutal one, the loss to the Houston Texans in their first-ever game—and he was cut.

TONY BANKS

He got only a $500,000 contract with no signing bonus, but he was hailed as the quarterback to replace Troy Aikman. He was dumped in training camp when Jones decided to go with rookie Quincy Carter.

________________________________.

The blank space represents the inactivity before the 1997, 2001, and 2004 seasons. How did that frugality work out?

- **'97:** Dallas wins its fewest games since 1989, missing the playoffs for the first time since 1990.
- **'01:** First year after Troy Aikman is gone becomes the second in a run of three straight 5–11 finishes. Put an asterisk by this one, though, because the Cowboys' salary cap was ruined by Aikman's departure.
- **'04:** Dallas follows a huge turnaround in the first year under coach Bill Parcells by sitting on its hands. All the gains of the previous season are pretty much wiped out as the Cowboys go from 10–6 to 6–10, barely better than before Parcells arrived.

But what was the worst? Considering how badly the Cowboys needed a kicker for 2006, signing the most accurate one in NFL history seemed like a no-brainer. Instead, they signed a guy with no brain.

OK, that's a little harsh. Mike Vanderjagt is just such an easy target. Truth is, he was more of a flake than a fool. And he was able to laugh all the way to the bank with his $2.5 million signing bonus.

The problem with this move is how poorly the Cowboys played the market. Adam Vinatieri was available, but the team hardly made a play for him, despite Bill Parcells having brought him into the league. Maybe Parcells's son-in-law, the Patriots' top personnel guy, tipped off Dallas that Vinatieri had his eye on replacing Vanderjagt in Indianapolis. Still, money talks and Jerry could've made a bigger play for him.

For a $3.5 million bonus, Vinatieri helped kick the Colts to the Super Bowl. For a wasted $2.5 million, Vanderjagt didn't even last until December. But amazingly, Vanderjagt might not have been the biggest waste of Jones's free-agent money in 2006.

Dallas gave Rocky Boiman a $1 million bonus, and then cut him before the season started. He wound up getting paid again by the Indianapolis Colts, where he teamed with Vinatieri on the Super Bowl champs.

**Attention, readers: I'd like to save room here for Terrell Owens. As tempting as it was to add him for all the trouble he caused in 2006, I couldn't do it because he did lead the league in touchdown catches. However, I don't trust him. So if he ends up doing something worthy of making this list, I've already got a spot waiting for him.*

WAS TERRELL OWENS'S FIRST SEASON WORTH THE TROUBLE HE CAUSED?

26 First off, he was to Jerry Jones.

The Cowboys made more than $10 million off T.O. in 2006, from jersey sales and other merchandise—including a $300 bobblehead—to the heightened interest he brought. You don't really think Dallas got all those great prime-time television slots because people wanted to see how Kyle Kosier was doing as Larry Allen's replacement, do you?

Still, this is an interesting debate because there are strong arguments to be made on both sides.

Yes, T.O. was worth it: He led the league in touchdown catches.

No, T.O. wasn't worth it: He also led the league in dropped passes.

Yes: Several of those came after tearing ligaments in his finger on one of the first few plays of a game.

No: Not the long, sure touchdown that cost Dallas a win

over Washington. Even Owens admits that was one he should've had.

Yes: The Cowboys still scored the fourth-most points in the NFL, an indication that having No. 81 around opened things up for everyone else.

No: Check the stat sheet. Jason Witten and Terry Glenn had fewer yards and touchdowns than the previous season, which shows that Owens merely sponged off them. The team's overall improvement on offense can be attributed more to the good health of Julius Jones and the development of Marion Barber III.

Yes: A-ha! The running backs had more room to romp because defenses kept safeties in the secondary to handle T.O.

No: Video proof, please.

With "Yes" unable to provide any, the "No" side gets to control the debate.

No: Explain why the hamstring injury in training camp took so long to heal and why team personnel weren't qualified to treat it.

Yes: Everyone knows hammys are tricky. And there was no point of rushing back in July when there was a chance of this becoming a season-long problem. As for the outside help, those folks have known him longer. They were the ones who got him ready for the Super Bowl in January

2005 when no one thought that was possible.

No: And the "Tour de T.O." schtick? That was a plea for attention if there ever was one.

Yes: It was funny.

No: There's nothing funny about an "accidental overdose." Lots of NFL players are given pain pills; few wind up in an emergency room because they took too many.

Yes: You're wrong—there was something funny. Kim Etheredge's line, "Terrell has 25 million reasons to be alive."

No: Love that, too. But what about T.O. falling asleep in meetings?

Yes: Has a doctor's note for it. And he doesn't like coffee.

No: He doesn't like Todd Haley, either.

Yes: True, but T.O. wasn't the one who put the rat in Haley's wife's salad at the fast-food place.

For every point, there's a counterpoint. That's the way Owens likes it—it doesn't matter what you say, just keep talking about me.

My pick? I'll go with "worth it," but not worth having back in 2007. (Unfortunately, Jerry Jones disagreed.)

IS BOB LILLY STILL "MR. COWBOY"?

27

You weren't thinking Nate Newton, I hope.

Lilly is the club's first-ever draft pick, the first person in the Ring of Honor and their first Hall of Famer. He's a Texas native who played college ball at TCU. He's still the role model for toughness, having missed one game in 14 years. He's still the symbol for quality, having made a club-record 11 Pro Bowls and being named All-Pro seven times.

And he's still the role model for competitiveness, best symbolized by him hurling his helmet across the field in frustration after the Cowboys lost their first Super Bowl title on a last-minute field goal. It wasn't just that loss boiling over—it was the fact the Cowboys had won the most games of any team the first five years of the Super Bowl era, but had yet to be crowned champions.

No other player ever has or ever will wear his No. 74. The last time it was worn was when he put it on again for the Ring of Honor ceremony in 1975, the year after he retired. (Among his gifts that day: a station wagon, a hunting dog, and a shotgun.)

A decade later, in 1985, the team honored him again by creating the Bob Lilly Award. It is voted on by fans for the player who best displays sportsmanship, dedication, leadership, and achievement. Troy Aikman and Emmitt Smith each won it four times; Tony Romo was the 2006 recipient.

About the only un-Cowboy thing Lilly has ever done is not cash in on his fame. Instead of going on the memorabilia-signing circuit or doing motivational speaking, Lilly devoted himself to photography. He put out a book of his behind-the-scenes Cowboys photos in the 1980s and has become an accomplished shooter of landscapes. He lives in Georgetown and still makes a few appearances, always introduced as Mr. Cowboy.

There really are no contenders to his throne.

Roger Staubach and Troy Aikman are certainly admirable, as is Emmitt Smith. Jay Novacek was all cowboy (lower case), but that's not the same.

Lilly was the right guy in the right place at the right time. The Cowboys might be lucky enough to one day have someone else who can be described that way. But no one else will ever rightfully be called "Mr. Cowboy."

WHO WAS THE HARDER HITTER: CLIFF HARRIS OR ROY WILLIAMS?

28 Roy Williams has built a reputation throughout the league as someone to avoid when you have the ball. His licks have put him into the Pro Bowl four of the first five years of his career. (It certainly wasn't his coverage skills.) He's blasted his way to all sorts of endorsements and a long-term contract, piles of money he dips into to pay off his fines for hits that cross the line. He's even got his name attached to a rule about tackling. The "Roy Williams Rule" bans jerking down players by the back of their jersey collar.

Oooh, tough-guy stuff. But he's no "Captain Crash." Harris played hard, but within the rules, launching himself legally. It was as if he had a big chip on his shoulder and was taking it out on every foe.

The Cowboys signed Harris out of NAIA Ouachita Baptist after he went undrafted in 1970. He not only made the team, he was good enough that Tom Landry felt comfortable starting him, letting future Hall of Famer Mel Renfro go back to cornerback. The Cowboys got to their first Super Bowl that year and won it all the following year.

Plenty of receivers from the 1970s recall a hit from Harris being the toughest shot they ever took. Legend has it that receiver Golden Richards, a teammate, came up with a great way of avoiding No. 43—he once brought a red fireman's hat to practice, having Harris wear it, with lights and siren flashing. Good pal Charlie Waters also tells a tale about the time in practice when teammate Craig Morton took advantage of Harris's aggressiveness by throwing a pass over the middle near the end zone, back in the days when the goal posts were on the goal line. Harris was so locked in on the ball that he lost sight of where he was and banged into the posts. Guess which one was left shaking. Hint: It wasn't Harris.

Harris could cover as well as crunch. Receivers didn't know if he'd try knocking the ball away or knocking them out. Sometimes, he hit so hard that he knocked himself out.

Harris made All-Pro four times and was voted to the NFL's All-Decade team for the 1970s.

He might've done more damage in the 1980s, but he retired after the 1979 season at only 31 years old. The human torpedo had fired for the last time.

Receivers everywhere had to be thrilled.

YOU ARE BUILDING YOUR ALL-TIME COWBOYS SQUAD...

WHO IS YOUR QUARTERBACK: ROGER STAUBACH OR TROY AIKMAN?

29 Staubach was the ultimate leader. He could win games with his arm or his feet. It didn't matter how much time was left, either, because he was "Captain Comeback."

Imagine if he hadn't spent those years in the Navy, which made him a 27-year-old rookie in 1969. Imagine if Tom Landry had trusted him sooner, rather than having spent those years battling Craig Morton. What if the concussions and other factors hadn't prompted him to quit following what was statistically his best season? Staubach really had only eight seasons in charge. Four ended in the Super Bowl. His title game record: two wins, two 4-point losses, both to a team some consider the best of all time.

He was the league's top-rated passer in four of his eight years—the first two and the last two. He retired as the highest-rated passer in league history and won nearly three of every four starts. But neither Roger nor Troy was a stat guy. The only numbers they wanted to be judged by were wins and losses.

In that case...

Staubach's teams never had a losing record. They missed the playoffs only once, then came back to make the Super Bowl the following year, back when such leaps were rare. Sure, he had plenty of talent around him. But there were several years he didn't have a big-time running threat. *He* was among the team's top rushers from 1974–76, the years between Calvin Hill and Tony Dorsett.

The old line in the Aikman-Staubach debate is that Troy was so good he didn't need to pull off the kind of fourth-quarter comebacks that built Roger's reputation. Aikman could make things look easy—robotic, even. He was a big, strong guy with a rocket of an arm and a terrific feel for the game. He went 3 for 3 in Super Bowls, earning the MVP award in the first one. He also won 90 games in the 1990s, the most by any quarterback in any decade. He could take a good team and make them great. The clubs from 1992–95 had the greatest four-year run in NFL history.

The only knock is that when the downturn began, he couldn't stop it. He wasn't able to take mediocre talent and make it really good. From 1996–2000, Dallas went 34–35 in games he started.

The pick here is Staubach because he found so many ways to win with so many different teammates. But you can't go wrong when choosing among two of the all-time greats.

WHO IS YOUR RUNNING BACK: TONY DORSETT OR EMMITT SMITH?

30 Dorsett always wanted Tom Landry to give him the ball more. That was never an issue with Smith. Dorsett might've been a threat to go 99 yards every time he got the ball, but Smith was a threat to get the ball every snap. His longevity, durability, and, of course, production vaults him into the discussion of the greatest running backs in NFL history. He's not at the very top, but he certainly belongs in the top five.

Dorsett belongs in that conversation, too. Like Aikman in the QB debate, he could be a runaway pick as the greatest at his position on almost all other franchises.

But for the team with the star on its helmet, the pick is the guy with the most yards in NFL history.

WHO IS YOUR NO. 1 RECEIVER: DREW PEARSON OR MICHAEL IRVIN?

31 It's funny that the defining moment of Pearson's career, the "Hail Mary," carries the lingering question of whether he pushed off. After all, No. 88 would become synonymous with shoves undetected by officials once Irvin started wearing that jersey.

Legal or not, Irvin's technique worked. He wasn't the fastest guy in the league but he was where he needed to be when he needed to be. On the field, that is. Off the field, he often was where he didn't need to be. But that's not the issue here.

Irvin is the pick because of his hands and his heart. He was as much of a leader of the Triplets and their championship clubs as he was a dominant receiver. He may not have a signature play like the "Hail Mary," but there were so many catches—the most in team history—that it's not really an issue.

And, since this is a mythical lineup, imagine how much better he'd be if Pearson was lining up on the opposite side. Pearson was Staubach's go-to receiver and was good enough to be voted to the All-Decade team for the 1970s. (Irvin made it for the '90s.) It's quite an honor considering Pearson made only three Pro Bowls. As mentioned earlier, this No. 88 belongs in the Ring of Honor, too.

WHO ANCHORS YOUR OFFENSIVE LINE: RAYFIELD WRIGHT OR LARRY ALLEN?

32 This is the toughest comparison because of how different the eras were. When he broke in during the late 1960s, Wright was considered huge at 250-something. In the 1990s, Allen was around 330.

Wright started out as a tight end and was known as the "Big Cat" because of his quickness. Allen awed folks because of how nimble he was for someone his size.

Allen is the choice because of his combination of speed and size—both his and the size of the behemoths he lined up against. Wright had to go against Deacon Jones and some other ferocious figures, but there were more beasts in Allen's day. And he was an All Pro whether he played guard or tackle.

One more thing about Allen: He was bigger and badder than pretty much anyone he lined up with or against. He could bench press around 700 pounds and go an entire season without saying 700 words.

WHO IS YOUR DEFENSIVE TACKLE: BOB LILLY OR RANDY WHITE?

33 White was a *baaaaad* dude. He remains such an intimidator that when he showed up at a November 2006 function wearing jeans while everyone else was in a suit, emcee Bob Costas sheepishly said, "I didn't want to be the one to tell Randy White he was dressed wrong."

But he's not the one called "Mr. Cowboy."

You can't have an all-time team without the pioneer. White might've ripped off more heads, but Lilly's talent was the foundation for this team, the driving force in the first Doomsday Defense. His toughness was legendary. His grit, too. But he was also quick and strong, perfect ingredients for a tackle.

The signature moment of Dallas's first Super Bowl was Lilly throwing his helmet in disgust after losing. The signature moment of Dallas's first Super Bowl win was Lilly bursting through the Miami line and chasing Bob Griese back for a zigzagging 29-yard sack. Lilly gets the spot.

WHO IS YOUR COACH: TOM LANDRY OR JIMMY JOHNSON?

34 Linked by their pair of Super Bowl titles, these guys are the biggest opposites on this list.

You couldn't go wrong having either one in charge. To try picking one, let's lean on an old line by the proud pop of current Cowboys coach Wade Phillips, former Houston Oilers coach Bum Phillips. Bum used this to describe Don Shula, but it works well for our purposes, too: "He could take his'n and beat yours'n, and then he could take yours'n and beat his'n."

By that measure, it's Landry.

Johnson was much more of a motivator than Landry. Tom has Jimmy beat everywhere else. Landry's Xs and Os innovations changed football on both sides of the ball. His playbook was a telephone book when everyone else had a leaflet. His game plans were as meticulous as, well, Jimmy's hair.

Landry was fortunate to have gotten a 10-year contract extension without having had a winning season his first four years. Team owner Clint Murchison Jr. believed in him and that was good enough. That faith ultimately was rewarded many times over. He also benefited from being able to focus on coaching, letting Tex Schramm and Gil Brandt take care of everything else. Still, he's the one who molded the talent they gave him into Doomsday and Doomsday II, and some great offenses. Johnson was just fortunate a former college teammate bought the Cowboys (even if Schramm already was eyeing him as a possible successor to Landry).

While Landry started from scratch, Johnson had a few building blocks. He inherited Michael Irvin, who'd played for him at the University of Miami. He was gifted Troy Aikman with his first-ever draft pick. A year later, he lucked into Emmitt Smith, whom Johnson knew already because he'd recruited Smith out of high school while coaching the Hurricanes. Then the Cowboys pulled off the Herschel Walker trade and made subsequent deals using their haul of draft picks. Dallas had so many that Johnson was able to throw a bunch of things at the wall to see what would stick.

A lot did. But Johnson didn't.

For all the talk about him being forced out at his peak, it's worth noting he never kept any coaching job longer than five years. Landry was in it for the long haul.

WHO, BESIDES THE CHEERLEADERS, INSPIRED MORE CHEERS: CRAZY RAY OR ROWDY?

35 Although the time Rowdy squirted me with a water gun on a 100-plus degree day at training camp in Wichita Falls actually felt pretty good, the mascot is ridiculous. He creeps out kids and pissed off Bill Parcells. (Oh, wait, that was actually kind of fun, too. It was great theater whenever Rowdy got within Parcells's sight.)

The concept behind Rowdy is flawed. These are the Dallas *freaking* Cowboys. They shouldn't need a silly character with an oversized head to get people excited. No, what worked for so long was an old man dressed up as a cowboy, waving a toy pistol and riding a stick pony.

Wilford "Crazy Ray" Jones started out selling souvenirs at the Cotton Bowl in 1962, using a whistle and all sorts of gags to entertain the customers. He eventually began dressing the part, wearing his trademark costume: cowboy hat, chaps, a patriotic vest, and a toy pistol.

He missed only a handful of games until bad luck and bad health set him back. By the 2000s, he'd been honored by a corporate fan-recognition promotion (the "Hall of Fans") and was instantly recognizable to anyone who'd ever seen a Cowboys broadcast—or to anyone who ever heard him whistle or saw him twist a balloon into an animal for a kid.

Any team can order Rowdy or his ilk from the mascot store. Crazy Ray was genuine, which is why he connected with fellow fans. He was a one-of-a-kind original, the kind every team needs.

Jones passed away in March 2007 at age 76. He took his love of the Cowboys to the grave, getting buried in one of his game-day outfits.

Maybe a new super-fan will emerge when the Cowboys move into their new stadium in Arlington. Better yet, let's hope Rowdy gets left behind in Irving.

THE MAVERICKS

DID DIRK DESERVE THE MVP AFTER WHAT HAPPENED AGAINST THE WARRIORS?

36

Hopefully by now your anger has simmered. You might still blame Dirk Nowitzki for the Mavericks failing to win a championship, or at least return to the Finals—or, at the very least, get out of the first round!—in 2007, but enough time has passed to reflect on the big picture.

Throughout the 82-game regular season, which the award is based on, there's no doubt he was the best player in the league. Kobe Bryant had more big games, Steve Nash had more dazzling moments, and LeBron James had more of a wow factor. Yet night in and night out, Nowitzki was the constant, the one whose team had winning streaks of 17, 13, and 12 games. The one whose team won 67 games. Simply put, he was the best player on the best team, with strong stats to back it up. While that's not who the award automatically goes to, it's usually a good place to start.

Had the award been announced right after the season ended, which is when ballots were turned in, there wouldn't have been much complaint. The problem was, the league likes to save the announcement until a few weeks into the playoffs. That's usually a safe move because MVPs tend to have deep playoff runs. Yet for the first time in 25 years, this MVP was already on summer vacation.

Even worse, the early exit was largely his fault.

Nowitzki didn't look anything like an MVP in the Warriors series. He had a few good minutes at the end of Game 5, but that only prolonged the inevitable, especially considering how he played in Game 6. There are plenty of reasons and excuses for it—many of them offered up by the big German himself—and that only made it worse, especially considering how far his reputation had come going into the 2006 NBA Finals.

Talk radio was filled with people looking to deport Nowitzki: "Two chokes in a row! The Mavs will never win with him! Where's Steve Nash when you need him?!" Suggestions were that Nowitzki should refuse the MVP award on the grounds that he no longer deserved it. Or that he should accept it wearing a Nash jersey. One of the funniest lines I heard was having the league give the award to Nash with Nowitzki's name scratched out and Nash's penciled in.

Actually, the award ceremony proved to be the perfect time to end the mourning, especially with most of the organization (including several players) in the room. There were lots of smiles and even some tears from team owner Mark Cuban. And Nowitzki was the one who kept things from being too lovey-dovey. He offered more frequent reminders about what he and the team didn't do than anyone else.

The guess here is that Nowitzki will come back more determined than ever. You can't work on leadership in his off-season German laboratory. But he'll come up with some sort of wrinkle to make sure he's still playing when the next several MVP awards are handed out, regardless of whether they have his name on them.

One is all it takes to forever be known as an MVP. You can't take that away from him—and you shouldn't even try.

WHAT WAS THE BEST CLUB IN TEAM HISTORY?

37 The good news is we can eliminate 24 of the first 27 teams pretty quickly, boiling it down to the 1987–88 version that went to Game 7 of the Western Conference finals, the 2005–06 squad that made the NBA Finals, and the '06–07 team that won 67 games.

Now we can throw out the '06–07 team as quickly as the Warriors threw them out of the playoffs. It gets tricky after that.

The 2006 team went a round deeper in the postseason than the 1988 club. But it can't be that simple. So let's break it down.

BACKCOURT/SWINGMEN

The '88 squad was loaded with Mark Aguirre, Rolando Blackman, and Derek Harper in their prime. Coming off the bench were Brad Davis and Detlef Schrempf, who wasn't the all-around force he'd become after leaving Dallas, but he was still a solid contributor.

In '06, the usual starters were Jason Terry, Adrian Griffin, and Josh Howard, who had a breakout season. Devin Harris, Jerry Stackhouse, and Marquis Daniels provided versatility and depth off the bench, with third-string point guard Darrell Armstrong making his best contributions in the locker room.

Advantage: '88.

FRONTCOURT

Smooth Sam Perkins started at power forward and James Donaldson hunkered down the middle. His solid presence was such a perfect complement to all the scorers around him that he was an All-Star this season. But the guy who really made this club go was Roy Tarpley. Before drugs got the best of him, Tarpley was a terror on both ends of the court. This season, he averaged 13.5 points and 11.8 rebounds and was named the league's Sixth Man of the Year.

With more talent than Tarpley and none of his personal baggage, Dirk Nowitzki solidified his status as the best player in club history with his best season yet in 2005–06.

Erick Dampier improved over his first season in Dallas, especially in the playoffs. His rise may have been sparked a bit by the presence of DeSagana Diop, who signed with Dallas after four years on Cleveland's bench and finally showed flashes of why he came into the league as a lottery pick.

Advantage: '88.

COACHING

Following the stunning resignation of Dick Motta, the only coach in team history, the Mavericks hired John MacLeod, who'd taken Phoenix to the NBA Finals once and the conference finals twice more. In 1987–88, his first team in Dallas won 53 games. His coaching staff included future Mavs coaches Richie Adubato and Gar Heard.

In '06, Avery Johnson completed his overhaul of the team's mindset, turning from offense-first to defense-first, while still managing to tie the franchise record with 60 wins. It also earned him the NBA Coach of the Year award in just his first full season. His large staff included longtime NBA coach Del Harris, plus Blackman and Davis from the '88 club, and even his own high school coach, Bernard Griffith.

Advantage: '06.

PLAYOFFS

In '88, Dallas got by a good Houston club in the first round, and then faced the best team in Denver Nuggets history. After losing two of the first three games, the Mavericks won three straight to reach the conference finals for the first time.

The defending champion Lakers, at the peak of their "Showtime" era, were waiting. Coach Pat Riley's bunch easily won the first two games at home. Then Dallas easily won the next two at Reunion Arena. Suddenly, the series became very interesting.

The home teams won Games 5 and 6, setting up a decisive Game 7 in Los Angeles. Whether it was the experience of big games, the home court again, or just too much talent, the Lakers turned a 6-point lead midway through the 4th quarter into another lopsided win. They went on to win the title, too—their second straight and third in four years.

The '06 club opened with a sweep of Memphis, setting up the showdown they'd been bracing for all season—their nemesis, the reigning champion San Antonio Spurs. In the best series in team history, and certainly the best second-rounder in league history, Nowitzki forced overtime with a 3-point play in the final half-minute of Game 7. Dallas went on to win in overtime on the road.

There were so many soap opera-ish subplots to the Spurs series that it would've been understandable if the Mavs had a letdown. And they did lose Game 1 of the conference finals.

But the big German would not be denied, not against old pal Steve Nash and a Phoenix team that had knocked Dallas out of the playoffs the year before. Nowitzki personally outscored the Suns in the 4th quarter of Game 5, and then led a comeback from 18 down on the road in Game 6 with a finals berth there for the taking.

The NBA Finals against the Miami Heat started off great, with Dallas winning the first two games at home then leading by 13 in the middle of the 4th quarter of Game 3. A 3–0 lead would've put the Mavs on the verge of getting to use the parade route city leaders already had drawn up. Instead, they lost that game and the next three. Blame the refs, blame Dwyane Wade, or blame the worst losing streak of the season. While it was still the best postseason in club history, the way it ended was brutal and bitter.

Advantage: '06.

SO WHICH IS IT?

The '88 team had more talent.

But the '06 club had more heart.

The '06 club all played with the spirit of their leader, Johnson, especially their most talented player, Nowitzki. That's why they would've won a matchup between the clubs, earning them the honor of greatest team in club history—so far.

WHICH WAS THE BEST "BIG THREE"?

38 The old-school Big Three featured Rolando Blackman, Mark Aguirre, and Derek Harper. The new-school version featured Dirk Nowitzki, Steve Nash, and Michael Finley. Sure, Nash and Finley were gone by the time the Mavericks peaked. Still, give me this trio any day. It was a team-wide lack of defense and weaknesses elsewhere on the roster, primarily at center, that kept the new-school Big Three from being championship material. Imagine what they would've done with someone like James Donaldson playing center. Better yet, imagine how Blackman, Aguirre, and Harper would've done with Shawn Bradley and stiffs like him in the low post. Aguirre probably would have forced his way out of Dallas a lot sooner.

Aguirre was the franchise's first superstar. First diva, too. His me-first attitude and a lack of toughness may not have been the reasons the Mavericks never caught the Lakers for Western Conference supremacy, but they certainly didn't help.

Aguirre, Blackman, and Harper can still be found near the top of every meaningful offensive list in the team record book. Considering their supporting cast, especially

Roy Tarpley, it's surprising the Mavericks didn't do even better before things fell apart.

Regardless, the original trio deserves credit for the Mavericks having been labeled the model for all expansion teams. But the new triumvirate deserves more credit for what it did. Especially Finley.

This team was worse than an expansion club when he arrived in the Jason Kidd trade. That deal began the dismantling of the Three Js, a threesome that had the potential to be on this list but is only being mentioned for a cheap laugh.

Another giggle-inducing memory from that era: Don Nelson once called Bradley and Robert Pack the "cornerstones" of the team's future. And that was with Finley already in place.

Dallas's turnaround can be traced to June 24, 1998, which might as well be a holiday for Mavs fans. That was when the Mavericks acquired Nowitzki in a draft-day deal with Milwaukee and got Nash from Phoenix. (Details in No. 3 of the opening section.)

The actual turnaround didn't happen for awhile. Get this: In their first season together, Nash and Nowitzki averaged fewer points than teammates Gary Trent, Cedric Ceballos, Hubert Davis, Pack, and Bradley! So nobody was marketing this Big Three just yet.

They finally clicked in 2001, starting a fun, four-year

ride. They made the Mavericks a high-scoring team at a time when defense ruled. Nowitzki and Nash became All-Stars, while Finley remained one heck of a player.

Part of the reason you rarely see three superstars on the same team is that it costs too much. Even a billionaire like Mark Cuban ultimately balked at the price tag. Right or wrong, he let Nash go. (Keep reading this section for more on that.) Then he got rid of Finley basically because a rule change let him.

No matter how well Nowitzki does with any other pair of sidekicks, it won't be the same. The nicknames Dirty, Nasty, and Filthy never really stuck. But Mavs fans will always hold a soft spot for the Big Three of Dirk, Nash, and Finley.

IS IT FAIR TO COMPARE DIRK NOWITZKI TO LARRY BIRD?

39 Both are tall and white and can shoot. Both won the 3-point contest on All-Star weekend, making them the two tallest winners of that event.

But let's cut it there.

The Hick from French Lick came into the league as a polished player, having honed his game while growing up in Indiana and in college at Indiana State, where he got a taste of the big time in the famous NCAA title game against Magic Johnson and Michigan State. Then he joined the Boston Celtics and took them from 29 wins to 61 and the conference finals as a rookie. They won it all the next season and Bird quickly morphed into Larry Legend.

The Wurzburg Wunderkind picked up the game as a teenager. He'd hardly played Division II caliber competition in Germany when he joined the NBA at age 19. Nowitzki began showing glimpses of his upside in his second season, but wasn't ready to become the main man for several years. He deferred leadership to Michael Finley all the way through the 2005 season. By the time he solidified his stature in 2006, he was 27.

So it's an unfair comparison. Bird was seemingly born great, whereas Nowitzki grew into it.

However...

The eighth season is an interesting dividing line in both careers. It is when Bird peaked and when Nowitzki took off. Bird went to the NBA Finals for the last time in his eighth year. The Celtics lost, leaving him 3–2 in championship appearances. Nowitzki made his first NBA Finals in his eighth year. He lost, just like Bird did in his first championship appearance.

Nowitzki is still young enough and surrounded by a

strong enough organization that perhaps he can still match Bird's three titles. He's already one-third of the way to Bird's MVP total.

Back problems slowed Bird. Nowitzki has had some ankle issues, but never anything major. With good health, there really is a chance he winds up being talked about in Bird-like reverence.

Nowitzki is so dedicated to his craft that he finds a way to get better every year. He's not the caliber that passer Bird was (earning the point guard-esque compliment that he "makes everyone around him better"), and probably never will—but he's getting a much better feel for hitting the open man. And his defense already may have surpassed Bird at his best.

Another perceived knock is Nowitzki's toughness. Anyone who says that, though, hasn't watched him enough. He should've shed the "soft European" label in May 2001, when he recovered from food poisoning in time for a playoff game against San Antonio, then played through a knocked-out tooth to score 30 points in an elimination game.

So let's wait until Nowitzki's career is over, and then compare it to Bird's.

Some folks can't wait. Among them is Bird's former teammate Cedric Maxwell, who offered these interesting comments to Boston radio station WWZN-AM in March 2005, a year before Nowitzki led the Mavs to the NBA Finals.

> *If I had my choice, in their prime, right now, between the two players, I would take Dirk.... The simple fact is, from a physical standpoint, Dirk is a better player. Now his will, now, all the intangibles that you guys are throwing in, makes Larry Bird the better player. But from a physical, from a purely physical basketball....*

Here's one last tidbit in the Bird-Nowitzki connection. In 1998, the Celtics had the No. 10 pick in the draft. Then-leader Rick Pitino was poised to take Nowitzki except Milwaukee snagged him for Dallas one spot before. Imagine what the comparisons would've been like if Nowitzki had worn the green and white of the Celtics!

MARK CUBAN: PRO OR CON?

40

OK, haters, listen up.

When 2000 dawned, the Dallas Mavericks had just finished a decade in which they were the worst team in all of pro sports. No team that was around in 1990 had a lower winning percentage than this club—not in the NBA, NFL, MLB, or NHL. Put another way, the Mav-wrecks were the biggest losers in all of pro sports.

Now? They're one of the best.

Yes, the Big Three already were in place. So maybe the team was destined for greatness. But don't tell me that Mark Cuban isn't part of the reason. You can question his style, but not his passion. Or the results.

Cuban made the team matter from the start. He got them on SportsCenter and back into the public eye with stunts like signing Dennis Rodman, even letting "The Worm" bunk at his house. There were draft-day escapades, blockbuster trades, electronic goodies for his players. Remember the comfy benches and new bath robes?

Yes, he goes too far with his ref-bashing. You'd like to think officials would be above holding a grudge, but they're human. So it's possible the Mavs fail to get the benefit of the doubt sometimes—maybe even in overtime of Game 5 of the NBA Finals.

But, again, let's go back to January 4, 2000, the day the Internet billionaire went from owning season tickets to owning the team. Cuban as Everyman is such a great story that it's always fun to tell. He came up with money-making stunts as a kid, from selling garbage bags door-to-door to selling Cleveland newspapers in Pittsburgh when the local papers were on strike. He went to Indiana University because it had the cheapest price tag of the 10 highest-ranked business schools. While there, he bought a bar before he was old enough to buy a beer. He started a computer company in the early '80s, sold it for a million bucks, and tried becoming an actor. Then he and a buddy wanted to find a way to listen to IU basketball games over this newfangled thing called the Internet. That led to a company they eventually sold for a billion dollars—each. He spent a chunk of his share to buy a team that wasn't for sale.

Cuban had been going to Mavericks games for years, including those dark days at Reunion. One of his favorite memories is sneaking into the most expensive seats and heckling Robert Parish. Once he had the money to buy primo tickets, he was so obnoxious that players noticed. That's why when they were told a fan bought the team, some of them couldn't help but laugh that it was *that* guy.

And here's something else for Cuban bashers to remember—he could've cleaned house, but didn't.

With his deep pockets, Cuban could've gone out and bought any coach he wanted. "His people" would have been more accountable to him. Instead, he realized he had a good thing in Don Nelson, and then learned the league through him. Both benefited from the relationship. Unfortunately, it didn't end with hugs and kisses. But their parting wasn't anything like Jerry Jones dumping Tom Landry.

Cuban may bother or embarrass you with some of the things he does—or doesn't do in the case of an upcoming argument, the departure of Steve Nash. But that sure beats having the Mavericks bother or embarrass you with the things they do on the court, which was the case for an entire decade before Cuban took over.

WHAT WAS CUBAN'S FINEST MOMENT?

41 Love him or hate him, you've got to have a favorite Mark Cuban stunt.

Early on, he endeared himself to fans by lowering ticket prices, letting folks in free if they painted their faces, and giving away tickets to people who traveled to road games. He wandered the aisles at Reunion Arena seeking feedback and posted his email on the scoreboard to encourage more dialogue.

He quickly became a celebrity. He sang "Take Me Out to the Ballgame" at Wrigley Field and was profiled by the television news magazine *20/20*. He was photographed on the cover of *D* magazine coming out of a phone booth wearing a Superman T-shirt and had a lewd interview with *Penthouse*.

He spoiled players with goodies, plus upgraded the team's standards: Better postgame meals at home and on the road (where visitors sometimes got junk), nicer hotels, and a really tricked-out plane. He also upgraded the postgame meal for visitors because those guys would eventually be free agents and he wanted them to know that the Mavericks take care of their people. It's worth noting that most of these perks are now standard in the NBA.

David Stern and officials aren't the only ones he's sparred with. There were some hilarious, sometimes juvenile exchanges with journalist Peter Vecsey and with Lakers coach Phil Jackson. I still think it's funny that he once rejected Scottie Pippen's request for a tour of his mansion.

Alas, those aren't even the biggies. The candidates:

- The Dennis Rodman experience, from signing him to letting him live at his guest house. The Worm quickly wore out his welcome, but it was one heck of a tone-setter for the new owner.
- On January 4, 2001, the first anniversary of Cuban buying the Mavericks, Dallas lost at home to Detroit 107–104. Cuban thought officials missed a goaltending call that would've tied it at 106. So after the game he had the replay frozen on the JumboTron and encouraged photographers to take a picture of it. He told reporters, "The refs were pitiful tonight and I don't care if I get fined." He did: $250,000.
- The Mavericks weren't always a lock to score 100 points and win. So Taco Bell decided to commemorate those occasions by giving out coupons for 99-cent chalupas.

  The Mavs needed one more basket in a lopsided win over Cleveland in February 2001 to wrap up the freebie. So Dallas set up a play, which angered the Cavaliers. A shoving match broke out and Cuban joined in. He was fined $10,000—the equivalent of 10,101 chalupas. He also was suspended two games.

- Dairy Queen. Need I say more?

  OK, the details: Cuban was so angry after a narrow loss to the Spurs that he took on the league's director of officials, Ed Rush, saying that Rush "might have been a good ref, but I wouldn't hire him to manage a Dairy Queen."

  Seizing the chance for free publicity, the fast-food chain challenged Cuban to work a shift as a manager to see how hard it was. He gladly complied, drawing hundreds of folks to a Dallas-area location for the chance to be served a burger by a billionaire. He also was fined $500,000 by the league.

- In 2002, Cuban himself donned a referee's zebra stripes and officiated a Harlem Globetrotters game. Two years later, he was the player-coach for their foe, the New York Nationals.

My pick? None of the above. It actually comes from before Cuban bought the club.

On December 19, 1999, Cuban was the featured person in the High Profile section of *The Dallas Morning News*. It was a long article that essentially introduced the newest billionaire to the community.

The final chunk of the story carried the headline, "Is an NBA team in his future?" There was talk of him being interested in his hometown hockey team, the Pittsburgh

Penguins. Then the writer mentions Cuban's interest in "a certain hapless pro basketball team." Cuban comes across sounding a lot like he's offering a blank check.

The Mavericks weren't for sale then. At least, not until Ross Perot Jr. read that.

The deal was done two weeks later.

WAS LETTING STEVE NASH GO A MISTAKE . . . IF SO, WAS IT THE WORST IN TEAM HISTORY?

42 I remember talking to Mavs officials the day after Nash signed with Phoenix. You'd have thought a close relative had died. It was as close to mourning as you'll see in pro sports. I honestly think they were more depressed than after losing the NBA Finals. Maybe it was because of how stunning this was, like a lightning bolt on a cloudless day. Re-signing Nash and keeping together the Big Three seemed like such a no-brainer. He'd even promised to let the Mavericks match his best offer. Then a lot of things happened at once.

The Suns showed up on Nash's doorstep the second that free agency began. They offered a ton more money—and, most importantly, more years—than Cuban was willing to give. Cuban had been willing to lock up Nash for four years, with a partially guaranteed fifth season. The Suns promised six, and a lot more money.

Cuban didn't think Nash would be effective enough to earn his keep in 2009 and 2010. Cuban worried whether Nash would be healthy enough to make it through 2005–08, too. And, if Nash stayed, the Mavericks were going to have problems on defense, the area they were going to have to improve the most if they were ever going to challenge for a title.

But, still, this was *Steve Nash*, the engine that made the Mavs go. Dirk's best friend. Everybody's favorite little guy. Why worry about '09 and '10 when there were titles that could be won in 2005, '06, and '07, when he'd still be in his prime? Wouldn't that make up for the back end of the deal?

Nash sure thought so. And the fact the Mavericks didn't agree had to be part of his motivation upon joining the Suns.

It's more compliment than criticism to say that Nash upped his game to prove a point to Cuban. Everyone is driven by something, so why not show your old boss he was wrong not to covet you?

Nash's two MVP awards in his first two seasons away sure made Cuban's decision look bad—except for one thing: How many titles did the Suns win? None. Neither did the Mavericks, but at least they made it to the Finals.

The mind-boggling part is how good the Mavs could've been with Nash and Nowitzki. Add in Dirk's MVP season and these two guys have won the award every year they've been apart. They still have zero titles between them, though, prompting one of the great debates about "what might've been."

I think a lot of Nash's rise is the marriage of the perfect player in the perfect system. That wouldn't have happened here with Avery Johnson, at least not in the same electrifying way it's happened in Phoenix.

But it sure would've been fun watching them try.

Despite all that, losing Nash wasn't the biggest free agency foul-up Dallas has ever seen. For that agonizing story, let's revisit the handling of Sam Perkins in the summer of 1991.

Perkins was one of the team's most solid players during its first great era. The Mavs opted not to lock him up long term because they were worried about his knees. So he played the 1989–90 season under a one-year deal, ready to become a free agent.

Between his strong play and a rising market, the club wound up offering a better deal ($18 million over six years) than he'd requested the previous summer ($10 million over five). Perkins said no thanks, opting to see what the open market might bring.

A $20 million offer came. The Mavs had a chance to match it.

A gaggle of mistakes followed, from general manager Norm Sonju being on vacation in Austria to the notion they'd be fine with just Roy Tarpley. They even wrote Perkins a letter saying goodbye and good luck.

Losing Perkins hurt. Losing him to the Lakers hurt more—especially when folks realized his contract there netted him less than the Mavericks' $18 million final offer once you take out state income taxes and add in a higher cost of living.

Of course, getting to play with Magic Johnson and James Worthy was a nice perk. And leaving the sinking ship in Dallas was pretty smart.

The Mavericks still may have fallen apart if Perkins had stayed. But he left and the team cratered without him.

That didn't happen after Nash left.

WHO SHOULD MAVS FANS SAVOR BEATING MORE: THE LAKERS OR THE SPURS?

43 There's so much history with the Spurs: San Antonio's franchise beginning as the Dallas Chaparrals; the Mavericks' first game, and first win, coming against them. The Spurs also have been longtime division rivals and, as an elite team since the late 1990s, a big hurdle for the Mavericks in their rise back to the top of the NBA.

Recent history with San Antonio includes Michael Finley and Avery Johnson going from key parts of one team's lore to key roles in the other. And, of course, there's that whole Interstate-35 connection.

Still, there's something about those Lakers. No, make that, *a lot* of things.

The Lakers were the big dogs when the Mavericks broke into the NBA, having won it all the previous season. Los Angeles went on to reach at least the Western Conference finals the first 11 years Dallas was in the league.

That includes 1984, when they ended the Mavericks'

first-ever playoff run with a 4–1 smackdown. The most infamous moment in club history came in Game 4 of that series, when Derek Harper dribbled out the clock thinking Dallas was ahead by one when the game actually was tied.

In 1988, the Mavericks made it all the way to the conference finals for the first time. And the Lakers were right there waiting. Dallas won a thrilling Game 6 at home to set up a winner-take-all finale...then didn't win another playoff game for 13 years.

Part of the spiral can be traced to Los Angeles signing away Sam Perkins after the 1990 season. The Mavs front office was partly to blame, but that doesn't absolve the Lakers.

During those dark days, Dallas hit one of its many low points in April 1997 with an NBA record-low 2-point quarter. The Mavericks went 0 for 15 from the field, scoring only on a pair of free throws by Harper. The Mavs went into that quarter leading by 14 and came out of it losing by nine. The biggest slap might have been that coach Jim Cleamons said afterward, "I don't think this was our lowest point of the season."

You want low? The Mavericks went exactly 13 years between wins in Los Angeles, from December 12, 1990 to December 12, 2003. That included 26 straight losses—spanning two buildings, the Fabulous Forum and the Staples Center. Counting matchups in Dallas, the Mavericks were 5–46 against the Lakers in that stretch.

Shaquille O'Neal was a big reason for it. He had his way

with a gaggle of lousy Mavericks centers, so much so that Don Nelson invented Hack-a-Shaq to try slowing him.

The skid in L.A. nearly ended in December 2002. Dallas led by as many as 30 points and by 27 going into the 4th quarter. The Mavericks had the league's best record at the time. What could go wrong? Well, the Lakers pulled off the biggest comeback in their franchise's history while sticking Dallas with its biggest blown lead. It also was the second-biggest 4th-quarter comeback in NBA history.

But wait, there's more.

Remember how good the 2005–06 Mavericks were? You know, the club that got to the NBA Finals for the first time in franchise history, led mostly by its defense? They sure didn't look like it on December 20, 2005, when Kobe Bryant personally outscored the Mavericks 62–61 through 3 quarters.

In Dallas's amazing 2006–07 season, a raggedy Lakers team bit again, ending a 13-game winning streak by the mighty Mavs. Revenge came a few months later with a 108–72 win in L.A. It was the Mavs' most lopsided win in this series and the fewest points the Lakers had scored since moving to Los Angeles in 1960.

The sad thing is, this is a one-sided relationship. The Lakers have owned the Mavericks for so long that Dallas is nothing but another team. Or, worse yet, a patsy, the team's current success notwithstanding.

The Mavericks had a chance to make more of a name for

themselves by joining the Lakers on the list of NBA champions in June 2006. Painfully, you recall them being stopped by a team from Miami.

Their coach: Pat Riley. Their center: Shaq.

Ugh.

Phoenix, by the way, is a late entry to this category. It began when Steve Nash left Dallas for the desert, then won the MVP in his first season and knocked the Mavs out of the playoffs. It continued with Nash winning another MVP and the Mavericks ousting him in the conference finals. Things heated up with some exciting regular-season meetings in 2006–07, including a double-overtime thriller in Dallas.

Yet, for this category, longevity and bad blood are at a premium. So even though Suns-Mavs is the current thriller, it has a way to go before the satisfaction of beating Phoenix comes close to the joy long-suffering Dallas fans should feel when taking down the Lakers or the Spurs.

Especially the Lakers.

WHO HAD A BIGGER IMPACT: DICK MOTTA OR DON NELSON?

44

(Folks, just to clarify, we're talking Dallas days only here. What Nellie did coaching against the Mavericks in the 2007 playoffs is off the table for this discussion.)

Motta turned nothing into something.

Nothing would've been better than what Nelson started with before turning it into something special.

Nelson had the benefit of buying the groceries as well as cooking them, to paraphrase one of Bill Parcells's most famous lines. Nellie also got to hire himself as the head coach, having come to Dallas only to be the team's general manager.

In addition to assembling the talented teams in the early 2000s, he taught them how to win. He never got them into the NBA Finals—never got any of his teams in his long career that far—but there's something to be said about getting a team so good that people wonder why can't you win the big one.

Motta never lasted long enough to hear that.

He walked away after the team's first division title, a

decision that's still never been fully explained. Even though the Mavericks had just been upset in the first round of the playoffs, they had in place the players who would get them within a game of the NBA Finals the following season. And it's not like he was in trouble with the boss; team owner Donald Carter was counting on Motta being with the Mavericks for decades, like Tom Landry and the Cowboys.

Mr. C got over his disappointment and let Motta talk him into coming back a decade later. He wanted to see what he could do with the Three Js. He gave up once he realized what a mess it was.

Things were in even worse shape when Nellie arrived in Dallas from Maui. He made all sorts of trades, some practically for the sake of making a move. Knowing that he was undermanned, he tried all sorts of schemes to try winning games. Some of them even worked.

His disdain for defense ultimately caught up to him. To his credit, he walked away once he realized guys were listening more to his assistant than to him. His relationship with Mark Cuban was strained, too, but fans still love him.

As well they should. While Motta got the franchise going, it was Nelson who salvaged a lost cause and put it on course for the success it enjoys today.

One last, trivial-but-interesting link between Motta and Nelson: Both tried getting their sons to succeed them as Mavs coach. Neither got his wish.

Kip Motta left with his dad after the '96 season. His last NBA job was an assistant on his dad's last team, the '97 Nuggets. He then became a middle school teacher in Utah, working his way up to principal—and coach—of the middle school and elementary school.

Donnie Nelson served as interim coach when his stepmother was fighting cancer. But he proved to be a bigger asset behind the scenes, getting promoted to president of basketball operations while his dad was still coach and GM. That made him his dad's boss. Donnie remains in charge even with his dad coaching the Golden State Warriors.

OF ALL OF NELLIE'S WACKY MOVES, WHAT WAS THE BEST?

45 Once again, the disclaimer: The 2007 playoffs are not applicable; this is about what Nellie did for the Mavs, not against them.

Trading for Dirk Nowitzki doesn't count. That proved to be a brilliant move by Don Nelson, not wacky. (Although saying he might become the Rookie of the Year was a bit loopy.)

Trading for Antawn Jamison and Antoine Walker and

expecting five scorers to share one ball was a risk that didn't pan out.

Inventing Hack-a-Shaq was wacky—and wise.

But for just pure wacky, let's count down this trio of tricks:

3. HACK-A-WORM

In Nellie's first season coaching the Mavericks, he tried slowing down the juggernaut Chicago Bulls by fouling Dennis Rodman every time he got the ball. Seldom-used rookie Bubba Wells started and had the dubious honor of going after Rodman. He succeeded, to a certain extent.

Wells got his name in the NBA record book by fouling out in three minutes, faster than anyone ever had. However, Rodman—a 38.6 foul shooter at the time—foiled the scheme by sinking 9 of his 12 free throws and the Bulls easily beat the Mavs.

2. THE 1997 DRAFT

Nelson took Kelvin Cato at No. 15 and immediately dealt him to Portland for the rights to No. 18 pick Chris Anstey, an Australian tennis player-turned-hoopster whom Nellie dubbed "not a project," insisting he may already be the "best running big man in the NBA."

Nellie was going to take Anstey at 15, but figured he'd be able to swing this deal, which landed Dallas some cash and bought some room under the salary cap. The bizarre part was Nelson's answer to the question of why he risked losing the guy he really wanted for such a meager return: "I don't know. The intrigue, maybe."

1. ATTENTION FANS, FOES: NEW BOSS, NEW TACTICS

In only his fifth game on the bench, Nelson let everyone know things were going to be different around here with his plan for ending a 15-game losing streak in Utah. His strategy came straight from the playground: *Keep-away.*

Realizing his team had far less talent, he decided to try rattling the Jazz by shortening the game. Dallas players were told to hold the ball until just before the shot clock ran out. This '90s version of the pre-shot clock Four Corners offense was such a shocker that the Mavericks had a chance to win at the buzzer.

Down 68–66, Dennis Scott put up a 3-pointer that would've won it. He missed, of course, because this was still the ugly era of Dallas basketball. But it sure was a good try.

It's funny and somewhat sad to realize that any team had sunken so low that a coach would resort to such gimmicks. Once again, it's a reason to appreciate how far Nellie brought the club—and how good fans have it now.

WHO WAS THE WORSE COACH: JIM CLEAMONS OR QUINN BUCKNER?

46

Gee, this is tough. Do you pick the guy with the .159 winning percentage or the guy with the .286 winning percentage? Both did such a lousy job that neither has gotten a whiff of a head coaching job since.

Cleamons had the "better" record, winning 28 of his 98 games. It was a huge disappointment because so much was expected from him. He brought a championship pedigree, having been part of the two winningest teams in NBA history—as a player on the 1971–72 Lakers that went 69–13, then as an assistant coach on the 1995–96 Bulls that went 72–10. Having won titles with Phil Jackson also gave him instant credibility.

Cleamons blew it all by demanding discipline and the Triangle offense. Neither went over well with his already bickering nucleus, the Three Js. Players hated the offense and hated each other. Jason Kidd threatened to sit out a season unless he or Jim Jackson was traded. Cleamons, trying to lay down the law, basically said, "Tough."

The front office went to shambles, which left Cleamons in

on the decision making. That's how he had a role in trading Kidd to the Phoenix Suns. Soon after, things were such a mess that team owner Ross Perot Jr. realized he needed a real basketball man in the front office. That led to the hiring of Don Nelson, which ultimately led to the firing of Jim Cleamons.

Buckner won only 13 of his 82 games, which at the time was the worst record ever for a coach who lasted more than a half-season. His attitude also has to be the worst ever.

A former star player at Indiana, the only thing Buckner seemed to learn from his college coach Bob Knight was how to be a jerk. Then again, Buckner was treated so royally before he ever blew a whistle that his sense of entitlement was understandable.

Rick Sund had just taken over the front office and he'd known Buckner for many years. He pushed for the hiring so hard that when Buckner requested a four-year contract, owner Donald Carter gave him a five-year deal. Really.

Buckner also was allowed to take his time before starting his job. He got to spend the final third of the 1992–93 season working as a broadcaster for the Minnesota Timberwolves and on NBC's studio show.

When he finally arrived, Buckner went out of his way to alienate anyone and everyone. That included being rude to the local media at a preseason gathering meant to be a relaxing get-together.

You want reporters to think you're all-business? Fine. Just make sure your players can handle it. Buckner badly misjudged how his act would play in the locker room. Instead of using veteran Derek Harper as an ally, Harper was among the first to be alienated. Harper ended up getting lucky—he was traded in January.

Sund's hands were tied because he needed Buckner to succeed. And with a five-year contract, Buckner figured he had plenty of time. He didn't, except for going down as the worst coach of all time, for the Mavs and for all local teams.

WHO WERE THE BEST—AND WORST—CENTERS IN MAVS HISTORY?

47 This is almost a trick question because of the "best" part.

James Donaldson is the only Mavs center ever named an All-Star. The current duo of Erick Dampier and DeSagana Diop are really the only other candidates for a "good" list. So let's have fun sifting through the many stiffs who have come through town to try figuring out the worst.

- Start with Shawn Bradley just because he managed to stick around the longest. Can you believe he lasted nine years, playing 582 games—sixth most in team history through the 2006–07 season?!

- Next up has to be the duo of Bill Wennington and Uwe Blab, taken with the 16th and 17th picks in the 1985 draft. (The more regrettable decision from this draft was taking Detlef Schrempf instead of Karl Malone with the eighth overall pick.)
- Bang a gong in memory of Wang Zhizhi, who probably figured he'd be the best-shooting 7-footer on the club, until he met Dirk Nowitzki.
- A big ACC shout-out to Eric Montross of North Carolina and the Duke duo of Cherokee Parks and Christian Laettner.
- Danny Fortson belongs on this list. I'm leaving him out, though, for fear of how he'd react to the news.
- Oliver Miller wasn't a stiff. He was a tub of goo.
- If you remember Scott Lloyd and Tom LaGarde, then you've really been following the Mavs a long time.
- For more recent fans, test your memory with the name Lorenzo Williams. You may recall him being so thin that he made Bradley look like Oliver Miller.
- From the blink-and-you-missed-them file:
    - Mamadou N'Diaye, three games in 2003–04
    - Bruno Sundov, 17 games over 1998–99 and 1999–2000
    - Radisav Curcic, 20 games in '92–93
    - Walter Palmer, also 20 games in '92–93

- Darren Morningstar, 22 games—yet, curiously, 15 starts—in '93–94
- Jim Grandholm, 26 games in '90–91
- John Shasky, 57 games in '90–91

Yet I still haven't gotten to the slam-dunk winner. Hint: He was the very first free-agent signee in team history, making him Dallas's very first center. Need more clues? He was the center on John Wooden's final UCLA title team. He was drafted three times by the NBA, but never signed—until the Mavericks convinced him to leave Athletes in Action, a Christian touring squad.

The name's Drollinger. Ralph Drollinger.

Drollinger had the size (7 feet, 2 inches, 250 pounds) but not the interest. Or the health. He'd actually failed his physical, but was signed anyway. He played only six games in Dallas's inaugural season, 1980–81, went on injured reserve, and then became the first player in team history to retire.

His career stats: 15 points, 19 rebounds, and 14 assists. Those would be tremendous if they were averages; as totals, they're ghastly. As the first Mavs center, Drollinger set the bar low. Sadly, he also started a trend.

SHOULD THE MAVS HAVE TAKEN GRANT HILL INSTEAD OF JASON KIDD?

48

Nope. Didn't make sense then. Doesn't make sense now.

Some folks were into choosing Hill with the No. 2 pick of the 1994 draft because of the connection with his dad, a beloved former Cowboys running back. Some liked him because he was a Duke guy. Others saw him as being less of a character risk than Kidd. (Remember, this was shortly after Michael Irvin's off-field problems had begun making potential sainthood a big issue for all local athletes, especially draft candidates.)

The thing is, Hill played small forward. And Dallas already had Jamal Mashburn. Maybe he could've been a shooting guard. But Dallas already had Jim Jackson. He wasn't cut out to be a point guard. And Kidd was as pure of a point guard as you could find.

When the Mavericks got the No. 2 pick, coach Dick Motta made it pretty clear he wanted Kidd. He said that when he came into the league in the 1960s, there were five great centers and five great point guards. He said the same was still true and he expected Kidd to instantly crack the top five.

Besides, with Jackson and Mashburn already in the fold, Dallas was going to be set at what's known as the 1, 2, and 3 spots. The grand plan didn't work. Kidd was the third of the Three Js into town and the first to go. Motta was gone by then, too. Still, that doesn't mean drafting him was wrong. As he might say, it was "most definitely" the right thing at the time.

WHICH TEAM LOGO: THE OLD COWBOY HAT OR THE NEW HORSE'S HEAD?

49 The hat. Without a doubt.

For more than two decades, the Mavericks had a unique, distinct logo—a blue M tilted to the right, with a white cowboy hat looped over the top right corner, all atop a green basketball.

OK, the green ball part was a bit weird. But the overall look worked.

The cowboy hat was a nice homage to the team founder and original owner, Donald Carter. Mr. C always wore a white cowboy hat, just the like the good guys in western movies, so it was a nice touch that his team did, too. Even Mark Aguirre and Roy Tarpley.

Original president Norm Sonju wanted a logo that would be distinct. His goal was for all sports fans to glimpse at the TV and instantly know they were watching the Mavericks, much like people can see a blue star and think of the Cowboys, pinstripes for the New York Yankees, and the skull-and-crossbones for the Oakland Raiders.

Sonju somewhat got his wish. The team's logo and colors smack of the '80s. And by the '90s, it looked a little cartoonish—like the on-court product at the time.

In 2001, the Mavs were moving into a new arena. An out-with-the-old, in-with-the-new theme was a perfect excuse for a uniform makeover. First of all, remember why teams change logos and colors: So you, dear fan, will spend more of your hard-earned money on their merchandise. No matter how many products with the previous design you might have, now you need to update your wardrobe.

Fine. But couldn't they have done better with the new look: a circle featuring a blue basketball on the right and a fierce-looking horse in silver, white, and black on the left. Look closely and you'll find a silver M on the black part of the mane.

The horse is a clever touch, except that the connection to the team goes over the head of most people. I mean, *you* surely know that, according to the Merriam-Webster dictionary, the word *maverick* comes from Samuel A. Maverick, an American pioneer who did not brand his calves and that the definition has grown to represent "an independent individual who does not go along with a group or party." However, the majority of folks out there don't have a clue about that.

My gripe is that the logo is not distinct enough. Unless you see Dirk Nowitzki wearing No. 41 or Avery Johnson talking to the guys in the huddle, nothing about it screams

"Dallas Mavericks."

The Mavericks had another failed attempt at shaking up their uniforms. Remember the shiny silver things that debuted in a season opener against the Lakers? They were gone by Game 2.

The alternate jersey now is a green one designed by P. Diddy. Used sparingly, it works. There's also something cool about the fact they read "Mavs" instead of Mavericks. Not many teams go by a nickname of their nickname.

IF YOU COULD'VE BEEN AT ANY GAME IN TEAM HISTORY, WHICH WOULD IT HAVE BEEN?

50 "Moody Madness" already has won the home category in argument No. 10. The road candidate is even better: higher stakes, tougher foe, way more intense.

In fact, what happened in San Antonio on Monday, May 22, 2006, has to go down as the best NBA game ever played in the state of Texas.

Let's set the scene.

During the 2005–06 season, the Mavericks won 60 games but the reigning NBA champion Spurs won 63 to claim the division title and the top seed in the Western Conference. All that work essentially was done for this, the chance to have a Game 7 on their home court.

Dallas actually could've won the series in five games, but lost in San Antonio. The Mavericks also missed a chance to end it in Game 6 at home, partly because they were without Jason Terry.

Why? Terry was suspended for punching former Mavs star Michael Finley below the belt during a loose-ball scramble at the end of Game 5, a play that unfolded so quickly most folks didn't realize anything had happened until the punishment was announced. Those dastardly Spurs knew it, though—they're the ones who made sure the league knew about it, too.

The punch typified how competitive everyone was. Having Finley involved was almost too good to be true for plot-thickening purposes.

Finley had been dumped by Dallas the previous summer thanks to the league offering all teams a one-time chance to get out of a bad contract. Still, Finley remained the highest-paid player on the Mavericks' roster—even after signing with the Spurs. You can be sure he picked San Antonio at least partly as an up-yours to Dallas, in addition to it being a good place to try to win a championship. Mavs fans reminded him of that with boos during this series.

Johnson's ties to San Antonio were even stronger. He hit the winning shot when the Spurs won their first title and remained among the most popular players in team history. He molded his vision for how to run a team during his years there and his mentor, San Antonio coach Gregg Popovich, always will be a close friend.

One last layer of intrigue came from Mavs owner Mark Cuban, who riled up folks in San Antonio by making fun of the River Walk. He also accused Spurs fans of being rude to his pregnant wife and he acknowledged cussing at dirty, uh, gritty guard Bruce Bowen after Game 6.

OK, on to the main event.

The Mavs made their first seven shots and started 17 of 20. They were up by 20 points before halftime. Everyone knew the Spurs eventually would rally and they did, going up 104–101 on a 3-pointer by Manu Ginobili with 32 seconds left.

Dallas needed a 3-pointer to tie it. Or a three-point play, but that seemed unlikely, especially since Popovich had just reminded his savvy, championship-tested players not to make a silly mistake like fouling anyone.

Dirk Nowitzki went for a quick layup anyway and Ginobili did exactly what he wasn't supposed to do. He fouled the big German, but not hard enough to prevent his shot from going in. A photo of Ginobli's hand grabbing Dirk's wrist is on the cover of a book called *Game 7*, which looks at all seventh games in NBA playoff history.

Nowitzki swished the free throw and it was all tied up again with 21.6 seconds left. Ginobili had a chance to still be the hero, but missed on a drive to the basket with about six seconds left. Tim Duncan got the rebound and Nowitzki got in the way of a possible series-ending shot.

Overtime.

The Mavs jumped ahead and were able to protect the lead, although it wasn't easy. They led by only four in the last 30 seconds, but hung on, thanks in part to some missed 3s by their old pal Finley. Final score: Dallas 119, Spurs 111.

Duncan scored 41 points in Game 7; it was his fifth 30-plus outing of the series after doing so only twice all season. Nowitzki outshined the two-time MVP, though, putting up 37 points and 15 rebounds.

This amazing series featured six games decided in the final seconds. Dallas won two in overtime and another by a point. Game 7 meant the most, of course. It sent the Mavericks to the conference finals and, ultimately, the NBA Finals for the first time.

It's pretty neat when one of the most important games in team history also is one of the best.

THE RANGERS

WILL THEY EVER GET IT RIGHT?

51 The Red Sox went 86 years between World Series championships. The Rangers are only in their mid-30s, so what's the rush? Just kidding. The point is, with this club, you've got to approach things with a sense of humor.

The latest rebuilding project is in the hands of general manager Jon Daniels. Yes, he's young—born in 1977, coincidentally the first great season in Rangers history. But Daniels's youth gives him the benefit of being less in a hurry than predecessor John Hart, who was always busy trying to make tee times.

Although Daniels obviously wants to succeed right away, he'd rather build for the long term than try patching something together. Far too often, that's been the Rangers' problem—a blueprint of trying to win now, tomorrow be damned. Previous GMs have loaded the lineup with bats and hoped to have enough pitching to make it through 162 games.

Doug Melvin was the first GM to try building the right way and was rewarded with three division titles in four years. Impatience about taking the next step proved A-Rod-iculous, setting the club back so far that owner Tom Hicks was willing to let Daniels try a new way.

J. D. is trying to spend Hicks's money wisely, not wildly. He's locked up Michael Young and is trying to build—not buy—a pitching staff. He also has "his guy" in the dugout, Ron Washington. The 2007 trade-deadline deals that sent away Mark Teixeira and Eric Gagne must start paying dividends in 2008, and certainly by 2009, if Daniels is going to keep his job into his mid-30s.

Before we move on to the rest of this section, let's take a quick peek at the silly past of the Texas Strangers.

This is a club that employed Jimmy (*Fear Strikes Out*) Piersall as a coach. They had Manny Mendoza in the lineup long after the "Mendoza Line" had become an accepted term for hitting futility. A few years ago, Hart's rebuilding plan included the addition of John Rocker, thinking there might be something left in his arm and kooky head.

Some other laughable, lamentable nuggets:

- When the Washington Senators moved to Arlington, the best player on their first team here was their manager—and he was 53 years old and a dozen years into retirement. Then again, he *was* Ted Williams.
- Years later, the team's best pitcher was in his mid-40s. Then again, he *was* Nolan Ryan.
- Perhaps the franchise's biggest claim to fame is a number: $252 million. Then again, it *was* Alex Rodriguez. (OK, that one was a joke. Remember, we've got to keep things light-hearted with these guys.)
- The first time they finished atop the division was 1994,

when a strike cut things short and wiped out the playoffs. They were 10 games under .500.

- There was a breakthrough in the late 1990s, with the Rangers winning the AL West three out of four years. Yet they "backed into" their first two, clinching them thanks to losses by the second-place team rather than earning it with a victory.

The Rangers went into the 2007 season with an all-time playoff record of 1–9 over 35 years. They also were on a nine-game postseason losing streak.

At least they had some company on the list of teams that have never been to the World Series. Joining them on the list: the Colorado Rockies, Seattle Mariners, Tampa Bay Devil Rays, and Washington Nationals/Montreal Expos.

The Mariners are the only ones in that pack to have ever won a playoff series. The Rockies and Devil Rays were born in the 1990s, so they get off a little easier—even if fellow '90s startups in Florida and Arizona already have won it all.

That leaves the Expos-Nationals and the Rangers. The race is on.

WILL A REAL ACE PITCHER IN HIS PRIME EVER PLAY FOR THE RANGERS?

52 Perhaps Brandon McCarthy will blossom into a legit No. 1 starter feared by lineups throughout the league. It could be Eric Hurley and his crackling fastball. Or Edinson Volquez and his confounding changeup. Maybe Josh Rupe and his wicked slider. And there's still hope that Thomas Diamond will live up to his sparkling last name, even if Tommy John surgery wiped out his 2007 season.

The key is that these guys are legitimate prospects. Not only are they the best arms in the organization, they're also considered among the best overall prospects in baseball. That's what I mean about building the right way—or, at least, trying to.

It generally takes four or five "can't miss" prospects to end up with one quality big leaguer. So the more pitchers the Rangers draft and nurture, instead of rushing them along or packaging them in trades, the more the odds will tilt in the team's favor.

McCarthy came in a trade for John Danks. It was a wise

move at the time, getting a more-polished guy also considered a heck of a prospect for someone thought to be a couple of years away. But, Rangers history being what it is, hold your breath.

One stigma the club has to overcome is the agony of pitching in Arlington. Free agents avoid the place no matter how much Tom Hicks throws at them because The Ballpark is so scary. Between dimensions that benefit hitters and heat that wears down hurlers, it's a tough sell. That's why no real ace will ever sign here. And that's why it is so important for a homegrown pitcher to succeed. He has no choice but to pitch half his games here, so if he can make it work, maybe others will think they can, too.

The problem is the "in his prime" part.

Should the Rangers develop someone, the guy surely will be smart enough to get the heck out of town as soon as possible. Thus, I don't see it ever happening.

WAS THE A-ROD SIGNING A GOOD MOVE AT THE TIME?

53 The guy was 25 years old and already a batting champion maturing into a potential home run king, maybe even the career leader. His talent made the lineup better, which was supposed to make the team better, which was supposed to help lure free agents. Rodriguez himself offered to be a recruiter. As if winning wasn't enough of a drawing card, his good looks and Hispanic heritage made him more of a marketing magnet.

The $252 million contract Tom Hicks gave Rodriguez made everyone everywhere take notice. Good or bad, no one was indifferent about this. The Rangers suddenly became a team to watch, drawing far more interest across the country than the once-every-five-days intrigue brought by Nolan Ryan. Like P.T. Barnum said, there's no such thing as bad publicity. Then again, Barnum also said, "There's a sucker born every minute."

I admit to being among those who thought it made sense. It wasn't my money, so I didn't see a down side to plugging the best all-around player in baseball into the middle of the lineup.

The mistake made by Hicks, and those of us who thought he was right, is that we were only looking at the good A-Rod could do. There wasn't enough thought to how teammates would respond to someone making *a quarter of a billion dollars*. There weren't enough questions about what kind of teammate he would be—or how he'd been before he was wealthier than many nations. There was no proof that A-Rod could lure others to Arlington, except the notion other free agents might think Hicks would overpay them, too.

And how could we believe there would be enough money left to pay everyone else?

Hicks deserves credit for taking a gamble. This wasn't as silly as the Mavericks giving Roy Tarpley a second, third, and fourth chance. Rodriguez was a proven commodity. But Hicks fell in love with the concept without truly considering the reality. That was as much of a mistake as the size of the contract—double the $126 million deal for Kevin Garnett that had made him the highest-paid player in U.S. pro sports. (Coincidence? I think not.)

Maybe a better debate is how things would've gone if A-Rod had signed for, say, $152 million. It's an interesting idea, except that Rodriguez wouldn't have come to Arlington for anything less than a king's ransom.

Hicks gave in because of something Jerry Jones often says when he overpays for a player: It came down to the question of whether he'd be OK with waking up the next morning and not having that guy on his team.

Fine. It's his money. And the idea of getting him here was right.

However, the price tag was so hideously wrong—enough to make this a bad move, at any time.

WHO WAS THE BIGGER BUST: A-ROD OR CHAN HO?

54

The Rangers lost 27 more games than they won during A-Rod's tenure, but it wasn't entirely his fault.

How about these feats from the back of A-Rod's baseball card, focused only on his three years in Texas:

- Won two Gold Gloves and an MVP award.
- Led the league in homers all three seasons.
- Led the league in runs twice, was second the other time.
- Finished first, second, and third in RBIs.
- Never finished lower than second in total bases, never lower than third in extra-base hits.
- Missed only one game.

Further inspection of his numbers isn't as flattering. He wasn't much of a clutch hitter, padding his stats in meaningless games, as the Yankees discovered. Still, he wasn't terrible.

Chan Ho Park was.

First off, this was a train wreck everyone saw coming. It was a panic move to try showing Rodriguez the club was doing something to build a pitching staff. Park was the best pitcher available in a horrible market. Overbidding again, they got their man—for $65 million over five years.

He did turn into a 22-game winner. It just took him 3 ½ seasons. Then again, a fly ball pitcher who lacks toughness and is comfortable as a middle-of-the-rotation guy shouldn't be thrust into the role Park had in Arlington.

The gory details from his baseball card:

- 22–23 record in 68 starts.
- 5.79 ERA.
- In 2003, he started only seven times—and won only once—because of injuries.

A-Rod was the bigger disappointment; Park the bigger bust.

WHAT WAS NOLAN RYAN'S BEST FEAT AS A RANGER?

55 Astros owner John McMullen thought Nolan Ryan was so washed up after the 1988 season that he offered to bring back the staff ace only if he'd take a 20 percent pay cut.

Washed up? Ryan had led the league in strikeouts the last two seasons. He was only a year removed from also leading the majors in ERA. Sure, he was going to be 42 when the season started. But the Ryan Express was still chugging full steam ahead, as the Rangers happily discovered.

What started as a one-year deal turned into five mythmaking seasons. Ryan went from a fearsome hard-thrower to a larger-than-life legend. And he went into the Hall of Fame with a blocky T on his hat. (OK, so it helped that he was under a personal services contract with the club. But still...)

Ryan was no 40-something part-timer like Roger Clemens. He went to spring training, pitching as often—and as hard—as his body would allow. And sometimes he did magical things.

Let's count down the six best.

6. THE 5,000th STRIKEOUT

On August 22, 1989, Rickey Henderson went down swinging at a 96 mph fastball at Arlington Stadium, spinning the strikeout odometer to 5K.

It was a bit of an artificial milestone. Ryan had long since broken the all-time record of Walter Johnson and already had separated from Steve Carlton to become the undisputed King of Ks. But a big number like that in a number-driven sport like baseball deserved big hype.

More impressive: Ryan went on to whiff another 714 batters, retiring with a record that will never be broken.

5. THE GRIT

On September 8, 1990, Ryan took a batted ball from powerhouse Bo Jackson off his face, but stayed in the game. He calls a picture of him on the mound in his bloodied jersey his favorite of his career.

4. THE 300th WIN.

On July 31, 1990, Ryan became the 20th pitcher ever to win 300 games, notching the milestone with an 11–3 victory over Milwaukee. He gave up just one run in 7 ⅔ innings, striking out eight.

3. THE 7th NO-HITTER

Yes, No. 7 comes before No. 6, even though this one goes down as the record. More on that in a few paragraphs.

Less than a year after showing he could still get 27 straight outs without allowing a hit, Ryan did it again on May 1, 1991, this time in a 3–0 win at home against Toronto. Eighteen years after his first no-no, Nolie faced only two over the minimum and struck out 16, including Roberto Alomar for the final out.

Silly sidenote: Ryan's no-no overshadowed Henderson becoming baseball's career stolen base leader the same day. Henderson celebrated by telling the crowd, "Today, I'm the greatest of all time." Ryan celebrated by riding an exercise bike and going through his usual post-start regimen, letting others hail his greatness.

2. THE 6th NO-HITTER

This is one is more magical because it was so much more unexpected. It had been 8 years, 8 months, and 16 days since Ryan's last no-hitter—yes, another of his many records, this for the longest span between them. Uh, one more: He became the oldest pitcher ever to do so, breaking an 82-year-old mark held by some guy named Cy Young. (Of course, Ryan would push it again a year later.)

This one happened on June 11, 1990, in Oakland, with a 5–0 gem against the A's.

1. THE DECISION

The choice here is December 7, 1988, the feat being the simple act of signing with the Rangers. Why? Because of the phrase so often used by the folks who ran the team back then: *He legitimized the franchise.*

Imagine a player going to Tampa Bay and bringing them respect. That's about what Ryan did for the Rangers, only they had a decade more of loser-itis than the Devil Rays have now.

Attendance spiked from under 1.9 million to over 2.1 million his first year, easily a club record. The turnstiles spun more than 2.4 million times his final season, with Ryan capping that year by taking home plate from Arlington Stadium to the new place. The Ballpark was still being built, but it may never have become a reality without the boost he provided to baseball in this area.

Picking Ryan's signing is a bit of a chicken-and-the-egg thing because it wouldn't have meant as much without the feats that followed. For instance, nobody considers the day A-Rod signed as much of a milestone—except maybe his agent, Scott Boras.

For on-field accomplishment, I'll take the sixth no-hitter because it showed he still had what it took.

WHO IS THE BEST PLAYER IN TEAM HISTORY?

56 You know where I stand on Nolan Ryan. But he was only here for five years, the last five of his career.

Ruben Sierra was on his way to owning this title, but didn't make it for a variety of reasons.

Rafael Palmeiro had some great seasons, but wasn't here for some of his best seasons.

Alex Rodriguez, Fergie Jenkins, and Gaylord Perry are all great players who did well here, but won't be best remembered for their days in Arlington.

Jeff Burroughs was the club's first AL MVP. Mike Hargrove was the first rookie of the year. Those guys, along with Charlie Hough, Jim Sundberg, and Buddy Bell, all earned a warm spot in the hearts of longtime Rangers fans. They just don't top this list. (Oddibe McDowell doesn't belong either, but it's just fun saying his name.)

Kevin Brown and Kenny Rogers are among the best homegrown arms in team history. But they also fail to make the final cut.

This question really only comes down to two guys: Ivan Rodriguez and Juan Gonzalez.

Both were signed by the club as teenagers in Puerto Rico. They worked their way up through the organization, and then they were the backbone of the club's best teams, the three division champions.

Pudge was the more exciting player to watch, among the most entertaining in all of baseball because of his passion and his powerful arm. Yet Juan was the AL MVP the first two times the team made the playoffs.

He's the one who drove in the winning run in *every* postseason win in the club's first 35 seasons. (Yeah, I know there was only one. But that still fits the definition of "every.") Besides, the Rangers always have been about bashing baseballs—and nobody in club history did it better than Gonzalez. His 372 homers and 1,180 RBIs are both franchise records. He's all over the single-season charts, too.

Look at the annual RBI list. Ruben Sierra set the team record with 119 in 1989, the year Gonzalez broke in as a skinny 19-year-old. He then matured as a slugger and obliterated Sierra's mark, knocking in between 128 and 157 runs every year from 1996–99.

I know what you're thinking about that maturation of his body, especially the timing of when it happened. But until the feats of Barry Bonds, Mark McGwire, and Sammy Sosa get stricken from the record books, what Gonzalez did stays, too.

One disclaimer to this pick: It's circa 2007. In a few years, Michael Young might shake up this debate. For now, though, it's Juan Gone.

WHO WAS THE BETTER CATCHER: PUDGE OR SUNDBERG?

57

This might be a generational thing.

If you followed the club in the 1970s and early '80s, "Sunny" is your man. He broke into the league as a 22-year-old in 1974, making the jump from Double-A ball. Made the All-Star team that year, too.

Never much of a hitter, he was such a great backstop that it didn't matter. He was widely considered the best defensive catcher in the AL in the 1970s, winning 6 Gold Glove awards. He even drew MVP votes in 1977 and '78, despite hitting under .300.

Sundberg left in 1984, but returned in the late '80s—just before a kid nicknamed "Pudge" settled in behind the plate. But Sundberg never truly left the Rangers. He's been involved in charity work and other aspects of the organization. The team named its community service award after him and he remains with the club as executive director to the president. The Rangers could do a lot worse than have a guy like Sundberg as their all-around good-guy icon.

However, the question was about the better catcher. And that's easily Rodriguez.

You probably knew that already considering he was a narrow second-place finisher for greatest player in team history. And you can make a good case for him as No. 1 over Juan Gonzalez.

Pudge arrived in June 1991 with a baby face and a rocket arm. He loved showing it off, too, throwing his way to 10 Gold Gloves in his 11 full seasons in Texas.

Like Sundberg, he wasn't much of a hitter—at first. As he matured (there's that word again), his stats improved. Rodriguez blossomed as a hitter in 1999, the year he was named the AL MVP and the Rangers won their third division title.

Questions always lingered about what kind of a signal-caller he was behind the plate, but the topic was balanced by the fact he wasn't exactly working with Hall of Famers. His arm kept base runners honest and his hitting more than made up for any other deficiencies.

Plus, his love for the game was so darn contagious. At his best, Rodriguez was the rare baseball player worth the price of admission. He might gun someone down at first base, or go full steam into second base on a ball hit into the gap. He'd jump up and clap his hands, his face going from intense to joyous.

You still occasionally see "Sign Pudge" bumper stickers around town, relics from one of several fan-led campaigns to convince ownership to hold on to their local treasure. It didn't work, of course, but things sure worked out well for him—a World Series title in Florida his first season out of here, then another trip to the Series in 2006 with Detroit, where he helped turn a young pitching staff into the best in baseball.

Good for him. It sure was great for the Rangers when he was theirs.

KENNY ROGERS: JERK OR JUST MISUNDERSTOOD?

58

For awhile, Kenny Rogers was one of the most charming stories in club history. Then he blew it. And blew it again. And that was before he blew his cool, leaving town with plenty of people not wanting the clubhouse door to hit him on the rear on his way out.

What a jerk. Bottom line.

Rogers was a short, thin, left-handed shortstop who also played some outfield when the Rangers picked him at the tail end of the 1982 draft. He left his family strawberry farm in Florida for a seven-year journey through the minors. Once he got to the majors, it took years for the club to figure out how to use him: Starter? Long reliever? Closer?

Rogers went from leading the league in appearances one year to starting 33 games the following season. He threw a perfect game the next season—which even earned him a congratulatory note from the "other" Kenny Rogers—then made the All-Star team the year after that.

Good stuff, eh? Here's where things start to go haywire.

Rogers's good buddy Rafael Palmeiro had left the Rangers in a huff with management; so when Rogers's contract expired, he bolted, too. The Rangers missed Kenny and Raffy so badly that all they did was win the division each of the next two seasons. Palmeiro returned in 1999, his feud over. And guess what? His pal Rogers followed in 2000.

Rogers left again after '02, and then returned in '04. It was the '05 season when infamy came calling. A preseason newspaper story said Rogers wanted a new contract or he'd consider retiring. He blamed the organization for leaking that story and basically decided he'd never again trust anyone in the organization or in the local media.

Anger suited Rogers—he put up a bunch of scoreless innings in a row. Then another snit with management sent his blood pressure soaring and he couldn't control himself. About a week after punching a cooler and breaking a bone in his non-pitching hand, Rogers decided to take his frustrations out on a cameraman who was doing one of the most trivial parts of his job—filming players coming out of the dugout and onto the field for pregame warmups. Rogers had made that walk thousands of times in his career. Yet this time he decided to go bonkers. He shoved one cameraman, and then went after another, knocking his camera to the ground and kicking it. That cameraman, Larry Rodriguez, wound up in the hospital.

There was all sorts of fallout: a suspension, a lawsuit, Rogers getting booed in Texas but cheered at the All-Star game. Crazy, crazy stuff. There was no doubt that the Rangers were cutting ties for good after this third and final go-round with the guy.

To his credit, he had one heck of a season in Detroit in 2006, perhaps again using his Rangers-fueled anger to prove a point. But whatever respect he regained, Rogers lost it all again when cameras zoomed in to reveal a smudge on his hand in the World Series. His benefit of the doubt vanished when Fox researchers found other video evidence of possible cheating earlier in the season.

One more point to consider: Think back to 2005, when Rogers was being vilified for shoving the cameraman. Around the same time, Palmeiro was being vilified for failing a steroids test. Funny that two guys who were once so close both turned out to be 40-something scoundrels.

Maybe Rogers is the kind of guy "you have to get to know" to understand. Sorry, pro sports doesn't work that way. You're known by the headlines you make—good or bad, fairly or unfairly.

Rogers knew the rules. He violated them. Often.

(Postscript: Even in June 2007, Rogers was still holding a grudge. After missing the first several months of the season with an arm injury, he coincidentally had his first bullpen throwing session in Arlington. In the locker room, he would only talk about it with writers from Detroit, insisting that local reporters leave. Grow up, dude.)

SHOULD RAFAEL PALMEIRO BE IN THE HALL OF FAME?

59 By all the statistical measures, he's a no-brainer. He's got both 500 homers and 3,000 hits, a feat accomplished only by Hank Aaron, Willie Mays, and Eddie Murray.

So? If it were up to me, the folks in Cooperstown wouldn't even let him buy a ticket. The only place they should post his photo in the hallowed building is at the box office, on a list like some stores have of people whose personal checks shouldn't be accepted.

Since I've argued this for years, I was always accused of having some personal axe to grind. Nope. I never had a run-in with Raffy. My problem is with his attitude toward the game.

This guy was all about stats, pure and simple. He didn't give a damn about helping his team win. He just wanted to look good. With enough pretty numbers, he figured his Hall of Fame ticket would be punched.

Well, not with this voter. (As a member of the Baseball Writers Association of America since 1994, I have a ballot.)

Back in the Cowboys section, I wrote about Deion Sanders being a mercenary. I noted that most pro athletes are, but that Sanders did so with such glee. Palmeiro is the baseball equivalent in the sense that he cared so much more about how he did at the plate than how his team did in the standings.

Yes, there are guys already in the Hall who got there by hanging on long enough to hit some big milestones, from 3,000 hits to 300 wins. Yes, there are guys who were me-first players from teams that never won anything. But Palmeiro never distinguished himself as one of the best of his generation. So why should he be among the best of all time?

Yes, he's got the stats. But they came in a statistically inflated era. And I thought that *before* he failed a steroids test, indicating he was as inflated as his peers.

At the time, few figured he was among the cheaters, especially not after his finger-wagging testimony before Congress. When that news came down, I welcomed my pro-Palmeiro friends to my side of the debate.

But back to the part about him not holding up to his peers.

Palmeiro was an All-Star only once in his first 12 seasons and just three times in a 20-year career. He was never higher than fifth in MVP voting, cracking the top 10 just three times.

Another slap in the face of real Hall of Famers was the stunt he pulled before the trade deadline in 2003. The Rangers were headed toward another last-place finish when the Chicago Cubs wanted to add Palmeiro for the pennant race. The Cubs, mind you, were his first organization. And we all know their pathetic history.

He could've gone to Wrigley Field and been a difference-maker. Do you know what it would've done for his legacy had he been a key part of their first World Series champion in nearly a century? Even if he'd only been along for the ride he still could've parlayed the ring into free drinks for life in any bar where there's a Cubs fan—and, c'mon, is there any bar without a Cubs fan?

His stance was that he wanted to remain committed to the Rangers. Aw, how sweet. To me that's just a commitment to being able to pad his stats on a team playing out the string.

He was going to be a free agent after the season and wanted to show how badly he wanted to stay. Well, if he'd really cared about the organization, he would've left so they could've added whatever Chicago was offering, then re-signed with Texas in the off-season. As it turned out, they ended up not wanting him back anyway. He wound up going to Baltimore, just like he did after leaving the Rangers earlier in his career.

The Orioles eventually sent him packing after the failed steroids test led to finger-pointing—not wagging this time, just pointing—at teammate Miguel Tejada. Real classy, Raffy.

Unwanted by any other team, Palmeiro was forced into retirement, beginning the clock ticking toward the day his name goes on the ballot.

If he does go in, it shouldn't be as a Ranger, Oriole, or Cub. His plaque should show him wearing a # sign on his hat and plugs in his ears, just like he needed to wear onto the field to try blocking out the boos he heard during his final season.

The people spoke then. Here's hoping voters do, too, when they get the chance.

WHY DID THE RANGERS RETIRE A LOCKER IN THE VISITOR'S CLUBHOUSE?

60 It was meant as an honor. Years later, it still goes under the heading "seemed like a good idea at the time." Except that it wasn't.

Here's what happened: In 2001, when Cal Ripken Jr. was on his farewell tour, the Rangers were looking for a way to pay homage. They could've gone with the standard rocking chair or the Texas cliché of boots, but that wasn't good enough for Rangers general manager Doug Melvin, a former Orioles front-office guy who had the utmost respect for Ripken.

But a locker? For a rival?

No way, no matter how beloved the guy is. Nolan Ryan had his jersey retired by three of the clubs he played for. But none of the teams he pitched against thought about making a special place for him, too.

What purpose could it possibly serve? Motivate the opposition?

With Ripken, the sentiment was heartfelt, as was the accompanying plaque: "This locker will forever represent the intensity, passion and excellence that Cal Ripken brought to the game of baseball."

Whatever warm fuzzies the gesture was intended to produce were gone as soon as the Orioles left town and a new club settled into the locker room. Realizing it, club officials eventually moved the display—which featured a hat, jersey, and some personal effects, like sunglasses—to the museum.

Melvin came up with the scheme by remembering his playing days, when a longtime Yankees employee told him about the hallowed ghosts that liked to hang around the stadium, and combining it with Ripken's greatest feat, the reliability of a guy who showed up to work every day.

As a concept, it works. So he should've shared it with his peers in Baltimore and let them do it in Camden Yards.

Not in Arlington.

WHAT WAS WORSE: GIVING UP ON A YOUNG SAMMY SOSA OR ACQUIRING AN AGING JOSE CANSECO?

61 Straight from the transactions file of your newspaper:

July 29, 1989

TEXAS RANGERS—Traded OF Sammy Sosa, IF Scott Fletcher and LHP Wilson Alvarez to the Chicago White Sox for OF-DH Harold Baines and IF Fred Manrique.

August 31, 1992

TEXAS RANGERS—Traded OF Ruben Sierra, RHP Bobby Witt, RHP Jeff Russell and cash to the Oakland Athletics for Jose Canseco.

By comparison, the Canseco deal looks shrewd. Sierra's career was on the decline. Patience had run out with Witt. Russell was headed toward free agency. So it was no big loss saying goodbye to any of them.

Taking on Canseco was a gamble, but one with upside.

He'd generate interest in the team, sell some tickets, and—who knows?—maybe even get motivated to return to his 40–40 form of a few years before. He was still only 28.

It was quite a change in thinking because in making the Sosa deal only three years before, Rangers general manager Tom Grieve's approach seemed to be "youth is wasted on the young." Why else would he have gotten rid of Alvarez, a 19-year-old, left-handed pitching prospect? Why else would he have dumped the 21-year-old Sosa after only 84 at-bats in the majors? That deal was iffy at best from the start.

Baines was 31 and already was pretty much strictly a DH because of bad knees. He was among the league's top 10 hitters—but that wasn't what a last-place team needed. They were supposed to be eyeing the future. They should've been the team giving up an old guy to get some youngsters.

George W. Bush was the team's managing general partner at the time. Years later, working a tougher job, he called this trade the biggest mistake of his adult life. (Debate any opinions you might have about that on your own; this is a sports book.)

Like the Herschel Walker trade, the Sosa deal got worse as time went on. By September 1990, it already was a failure because the Rangers dealt Baines to Oakland for pitchers Joe Bitker and Scott Chiamparino. They won a combined three games for Texas.

History really began working against the deal in August 1991. The White Sox had been smart enough to realize that Alvarez wasn't ready for the majors, so they sent him for some seasoning in the minors. Upon bringing him back to the big leagues, all he did was throw a no-hitter—in his first start. Alvarez remained a solid member of Chicago's rotation through 1997. He hung around the majors until he was 35, winning a total of 102 games.

As bad as this trade seems so far, we still haven't gotten to Sosa. Sammy actually was pretty unspectacular for the White Sox. So they gave up on him, too, sending him across town to the Cubs. You know what happened after that. His stay may have ended with memories of a corked bat, overly loud music in the clubhouse, and a generally bad attitude, but for several years he was among the most beloved players, and most feared hitters, in all of baseball.

There's no telling what Alvarez or Sosa would've done had they remained with the Rangers. But don't you wish they had found out?

IF YOU COULD'VE BEEN AT ANY GAME IN TEAM HISTORY, WHICH WOULD IT HAVE BEEN?

62 Going into the 2007 season, there had been only one playoff win. While its singular status makes it memorable, it's not exactly wish-I'd-been-there quality. Nolan Ryan provided a bunch of those. In a strange way, maybe too many. It's hard to pick just one, although both no-hitters are great choices.

A perfect game, though, is the perfect choice. (And, no, not the one Mike Witt threw against Texas on the final day of the 1984 season.) What Kenny Rogers did July 28, 1994—facing 27 batters and retiring them all—is among the greatest individual performances among all local teams.

One of the charming side notes is that Rogers didn't even realize what he'd done. He knew it was a no-hitter, but he wasn't even familiar with the term "perfect game." His was the 14th in baseball history, the first by an AL lefty.

Rogers threw just 98 pitches. Bo Jackson whiffed in all three of his at-bats, but Rogers was so efficient that he only fanned eight. A solo home run by Jose Canseco and an RBI single by

Dean Palmer gave Rogers a 2–0 lead after 1 inning.

The closest Rogers came to putting anyone on base was the 7th inning, when he went to three-ball counts on all three batters. The closest anyone came to a hit was Rex Hudler at the start of the 9th. He hit a sinking line drive that Rusty Greer, then a rookie, snagged with a tremendous, all-out diving catch. Greer had a much easier catch for the final out.

In only his second season as a starter, Rogers went into this game in a rut. He'd been roughed up in his last few starts. His shoulder had been hurting, too. Yet everything clicked that night, providing a bright spot on a day marred by baseball players having set a strike date. There was even a record crowd at The Ballpark in Arlington: 46,581 filling the first-year stadium on a Thursday night.

It was...perfect.

RANGERS UNIFORMS: RED OR BLUE?

63 Before The Ballpark opened in 1994, stadium architect David Schwarz excitedly talked about the red accents throughout the building that were supposed to be brought out by the team's new color scheme. Or maybe it was the other way around—the uniforms highlighted by the accents.

Whatever. It worked. There was just something that clicked when the Rangers broke out the red hats, red shoes, and red-lettered uniforms.

By 2001, it was time for a change. Back to blue. And you know what? It was time. Red was good, but it had run its course.

Overall, Rangers fans have been lucky from a sartorial perspective. The club started with red, white, and blue and has stuck with it, changing the look every so often but almost always for the better.

The initial logo—a baseball wearing an oversized cowboy hat—seems goofy now but it was apropos in its time, 1972–82.

The iconic shape of the state of Texas was featured next. The '83 version was poorly executed, so a new version was made for '84. It lasted all the way until the new stadium demanded a new look.

The Texas flag was added as a patch in 2001, another nice

touch. And the latest logo, unveiled in '03, is the cleanest yet—a baseball with a red T, the full name in a circle around it all.

The red look was good in its day, but the blue styles are far superior now.

The Rangers haven't always pitched well or played very good defense. But at least they've always had above-average uniforms.

WHO IS THE RANGERS' BIGGEST RIVAL?

64 The Rangers had the misfortune of becoming a playoff regular about the same time as the latest Yankees dynasty was heating up. Texas had a chance to get in New York's way. The Rangers even got off to a 1–0 start in the 1996 series. But the Yankees came back by winning the next nine, counting sweeps in 1997 and '99. While that's a good reason to hold a grudge, it's not enough to build a rivalry.

So maybe it should be a division foe. But, which one?

Oakland has been the best lately, but wasn't much of a factor in the years the Rangers were rolling. Seattle has been around the shortest time and done the least damage—unless you want to blame the Mariners for A-Rod, since that's where he played before coming to Texas.

How about the Angels, from whatever city or state they're currently named after? There's been some bad blood in recent years, which could be the start of something interesting between the teams. It's just not there yet.

Then who is it? It can't be the Astros, even if there is that contrived Silver Boot thing. Seems to me that there isn't one, not a really good one.

So how about this:

Since a real rivalry means "rooting for the Rangers and whoever is playing (the rivals)," how about Texas fans cheering against anything good happening to the Mariners, Colorado Rockies, Tampa Bay Devil Rays, and Washington Nationals.

Like the Rangers, those clubs have never been to a World Series. No reason any of them should get there first, either.

WHAT'S THE MOST BIZARRE SLICE OF TEAM HISTORY?

65 Ahh. Finally a chance for the Rangers to distinguish themselves.

Lots of teams can pitch, play defense, and hit. Few teams can offer the kind of extra-curricular entertainment this club has since moving to Arlington in 1972.

Before I pick my bizarro favorito, let's review some of the candidates:

THE ROOKIE

The first sellout in team history was in 1973 for the debut of David Clyde.

Only 20 days removed from his final high school outing, the ink barely dry on his record $125,000 signing bonus for being the No. 1 overall pick in the draft, Clyde skipped the minors and was sent straight to the mound for his major league debut.

So many people wanted to be there that the first pitch was delayed until the mess in the parking lot got cleared up. He won the game, but would win only six more for the Rangers. Clyde won only 18 games over his big-league career, which ended when he was only 26.

TAKE THIS JOB AND SHOVE IT, PART I

Future coach-choker Latrell Sprewell was only 6 years old when the Rangers had their own player revolt.

In the laid-back environment of spring training in 1977, Lenny Randle heard that manager Frank Lucchesi was bad-mouthing him—and planning to bench him—so the 25-year-old Randle sucker-punched the 50-year-old Lucchesi, knocking him to the ground, then wailed away some more.

Lucchesi broke his cheekbone, cut his lip, and got a concussion. Randle was fined $10,000, suspended for 30 days, and traded to the Mets before ever getting back on the field for Texas. Lucchesi was fired after 62 games and wound up suing Randle; he got an out-of-court settlement.

TAKE THIS JOB AND SHOVE IT, PART II

Later that same summer, Eddie Stanky decided he wasn't cut out to manage any more, so he quit. After one game. At least his 1.000 winning percentage is an unbreakable team record. Although, in typical Rangers fashion, he's not the only one to have worked only one day. Del Wilber did so in 1973, holding down the fort after Whitey Herzog was fired and before Billy Martin took over. So he, too, is permanently 1–0.

The difference in their 24-hour tenures is that it was Wilber's one and only game as a big-league skipper. Stanky had managed before, so he knew what he was getting into. In fact, that's probably why he quit.

WHAT WAS HE THINKING? PART I.

At the risk of setting off the Politically Correct police, the following mental health-related incident still fits here because, well, it's so bizarre. In 1978, relief pitcher Roger Moret was found in a catatonic state in the locker room. He was frozen, staring at a shower shoe—for two hours!

WHAT WAS HE THINKING? PART II

In 1985, two days before he was honored with the club's "Good Guy" award, pitcher Dave Stewart is arrested in Los Angeles and charged with lewd conduct. This conduct was performed with a 6-foot, 3-inch prostitute named Lucille who, beneath female clothing, actually was a guy named Elson Tyler.

The most amazing part of this story is that Stewart still showed up to collect his award in front of his bosses, his teammates, fans, and even AL president Bobby Brown. Stewart won the award for always being accommodating and professional. He proved it again by showing up.

WHAT WAS HE THINKING? PART III

Frank Francisco is young, so maybe he'll do some good deed to overcome the bad one the night of September 13, 2004.

Sitting in the bullpen along the right-field foul line in Oakland, all Rangers relievers were getting heckled by the fans. How far over the line the screamers went doesn't really matter—not after Francisco picked up a metal chair and hurled it into the crowd, breaking the nose and cutting the face of a woman whose husband was the target. (He had ducked.)

Joke all you want about a Rangers pitcher missing the target or about the woman already suffering enough by being married to that guy. Bottom line is, this is one of the worst incidents in club history.

Others receiving votes:

- The Rangers won a 1974 game in Cleveland by forfeit, thanks to a failed promotion called Ten-Cent Beer Night. Actually, failed is the wrong word. It actually proved to be too popular. Drunk fans swarmed the field, wielding all sorts of makeshift weapons as they charged at Texas players.

- Billy Martin capped the first season with the designated hitter (1974) by letting Ferguson Jenkins hit for himself. It was a good call as Fergie got the team's first hit and won the game, earning his still-club-record 25th victory of the year.
- In spring training of 1986, rookie Pete Incaviglia hit a ball *through* the outfield fence.
- In April 1986, Bobby Witt was pulled from the second start of his career after giving up 2 runs, with 8 walks and 4 wild pitches. The strange part? He hadn't allowed a hit! He'd also struck out 10. It's doubtful another pitcher has been pulled with a 10-K no-hitter going.

THE WINNER: A DOUBLE-HEADER (SORT OF), STARRING JOSE CANSECO

Three days apart in 1993, Canseco did a pair of unimaginable things that underscored what a circus act his life had become—and, in a way, spoke volumes about the Rangers.

It started in Cleveland, with Canseco, out in his customary spot in right field, clumsily tracking a fly ball hit by Carlos Martinez. Canseco was poised to catch it on the warning track. Instead, the ball caught him on the noggin and bounced over the fence for a home run.

Then, in Boston, the Rangers were getting routed by the

Red Sox. Apparently already over the embarrassment of what had happened in Cleveland, Canseco begged manager Kevin Kennedy to let him pitch. More amazingly, Kennedy let him. Canseco's line: 2 hits, 3 walks, 3 runs, and 1 torn elbow ligament.

From insult to injury, Canseco gave it all to the club in less than a week. It was only May and they were without their supposedly superstar slugger for the rest of the season.

Let's end this section with a final, fitting tidbit, shared in the form of a trivia question: What was the last name of "Doug -------," a journeyman infielder who played for seven teams from 1989–98, but played the majority of his big-league games for the Texas Rangers?

Strange.

THE STARS

CAN DALLAS BE CALLED A HOCKEY TOWN?

66 "Hockeytown?" Hardly. But a hockey town? You bet. As long as the Stars are winning and the team's marketing folks are, too.

My definition of being a hockey town is supporting the local team. Dallas–Fort Worth fans pass that test, providing the team gives them something to cheer about and the promoters keep making "the hottest game on ice" the place to be.

It's not blind loyalty. It's a relationship contingent on winning or at least providing good bang for the entertainment buck. Give us a quality product and we'll show you the money. What more can you expect in an area where most people did not grow up playing or following the sport? Folks here don't watch "Hockey Night in Canada." Most either don't have or don't watch Versus. (Don't feel bad if you are reading this and don't know that Versus is the satellite network that carries NHL games; the ratings show there are a lot of folks out there just like you.)

In the early days of the NHL in Big D, the theory was that there were about 10,000 die-hard hockey fans here, many of them transplants. Others were sold on the game with the concept of it being "football on ice," which is why goon

Shane Churla might've been the most popular player that first season.

From the start, the Stars were smart enough to recognize the need to make sure everyone who grew up in Dallas was exposed to hockey at a young age. The team's devotion to youth hockey eventually will pay off with lifelong puck-heads. But that takes a generation.

So, for their first decade-plus, the organization (remember, in hockey terms, that's pronounced or-gan-*eye*-ZAY-shun) has filled the stands by making their games a hot ticket, whether it's chasing championships or drawing in beautiful people.

A decline in the standings while prices were going up was a bad combination. The lockout deepened the divide. But the Stars have done a decent job of winning fans back.

It remains to be seen how the economy will support the Stars and Mavs having long runs the same spring-summer. It takes a lot of money to buy playoff-priced tickets for both teams in April, May, and June. The Mavs will sell out first. But I predict the Stars wouldn't be left with any empties either.

After all, this is a hockey town.

AFTER MIKE MODANO, WHO IS THE NO. 2 STAR?

67 Mike Modano is a lock for No. 1, so let's discuss the runner-up.

It sure is tempting to pick the guy who wore No. 2 with distinction, former captain Derian Hatcher. When Hatcher was on the ice, the guys in the opposing sweater knew they had to keep an eye on No. 2. Not that it was difficult—at 6 feet, 5 inches, and 235 pounds, he was easy to spot.

Hatcher was the eighth overall pick in the 1990 NHL entry draft. His third full season was the team's first in Dallas, so he sort of came of age before the fans' eyes. He donned the captain's C on his sweater in 1995 at only 23 years old. A few years later he became the first American-born captain of a Stanley Cup champion. By the time he left as a free agent, Hatcher had played 12 seasons for the club, 10 in Dallas. He'd played the third-most games in team history and was third in penalty minutes.

Yet Hatcher is the third star on my list, behind Joe Nieuwendyk.

The argument starts with one undeniable factor in Joe's

favor: He was the postseason MVP of the team's first Stanley Cup championship. It says so right there on the Conn Smythe Trophy, a reward for having scored 11 goals, including the winner in 6 of Dallas's 16 victories.

Nieuwendyk was a perfect complement to Modano, a second elite center for teams to try to control in a pick-your-poison sort of way. Though he was only here less than seven full seasons, they were some of the best in club history and he was a big reason why.

His impact on the organization (you are pronouncing it hockey-style by now, right?) went beyond his 178 goals, among the top 10 in franchise history, and his 35 game-winners, third most in franchise history.

See, Nieuwendyk was a respected player before he arrived in Dallas, having helped Calgary win the Stanley Cup in 1989. And even though the Stars gave up a future All-Star in Jarome Iginla to get Nieuwendyk, his bad back and big contract, his arrival was the first proof that the Stars were serious about building a winner down south. It's fair to say he brought some of the same kind of credibility to the Stars that Nolan Ryan brought when he joined the Rangers.

Consider these things, which might be coincidences as isolated events, but taken together seem more like a pattern:

- The Stars won their first division title in Dallas in Nieuwendyk's first full season here. In fact, they won division titles in all five of his full seasons here.

- In 1998, the year before the Stars won the Cup, they lost the conference finals to Detroit in six games. Nieuwendyk, however, missed the Red Wings series with a knee injury suffered the previous round on a cheap shot by Edmonton's Bryan Marchment. If Nieuwendyk could've been in the lineup playing anywhere near as good as he did the following post-season, the Stars might've brought home the Cup a year earlier.
- The trade of Nieuwendyk and Jamie Langenbrunner remains a dark day in recent Stars history. Even darker was the club winning only one playoff series from the time he left until he retired.

This ranking, of course, is subject to change as time goes on. Jere Lehtinen and Sergei Zuboz are quality, consistent performers who could nudge their way into the conversation with a few more good years. However, my early favorite is the current captain, Brenden Morrow. And don't write off Marty Turco just yet either. (If you do, then add Mike Smith to the list in case he becomes the goalie of the future.)

BELFOUR OR TURCO?

68 To quote one of the greatest fan chants ever heard in these parts: "Ed-die's Bet-ter!" And Belfour didn't even bribe me a billion bucks to say that.

Belfour was a weird guy, but the Eagle could be special when it mattered most. He was the right guy between the pipes on a team with enough strong personalities in the dressing room that his antics could be ignored.

Belfour was as big of a reason as any why the Stars got to the Western Conference finals in 1998, why they won the Stanley Cup in 1999, and why they got back to the Stanley Cup finals in 2000.

Considering that Belfour was signed before the '98 season to get this club to new heights, he probably should be listed in the sections of this book about greatest free-agent signings among all local teams.

But signing him was risky, not glitzy. It was more along the lines of the Cowboys adding Charles Haley, another guy who came in with the ability to dominate but only if he put aside his locker-room and off-field issues long enough.

Fans' appreciation for Belfour came pouring out during Game 7 of the 2000 Western Conference finals. Reunion Arena was seldom louder than when 17,001 Stars fans let Colorado's

Patrick Roy hear their pick as the top goaltender with their cries of "Ed-die's Bet-ter!" Sure, the scoreboard already showed that. But the way they rubbed it in was classic.

Adding to Belfour's legend was what happened on a March night in 2000 at the ritzy Mansion hotel. The details include frightening his date, brawling with a security guard, the use of pepper spray to subdue him, and then an offer of $1 billion if cops would let him go. He eventually was sentenced to two years' probation, fined $3,000, and told to visit schools to warn kids about the dangers of alcohol abuse.

Belfour wore out his welcome soon enough, in part because the club thought they really had something special in Marty Turco.

The problem is, Turco's greatest games have been in the regular season.

In his first year as the starter, Turco broke an ancient NHL record for the lowest goals-against average. That impressive mark would've meant a heck of a lot more if the Stars had done anything in the playoffs. Instead, they were KO'd in the second round.

A year later, they were ousted by Colorado in the first round, in five games. After the lockout, the exact same thing happened: A five-game, first-round ousting by Colorado.

Turco had another good regular season in 2006–07, becoming the winningest goalie in franchise history, yet he also had an up-and-coming backup in Mike Smith. He knew the pressure was on in the playoffs—and he responded in a big way.

Although Dallas lost to Vancouver in the first round, the series went seven games thanks to 3 shutouts by Turco. Put another way, the only times the Stars won was when the Canucks didn't score. He had a scoreless stretch of 165 minutes and 45 seconds, breaking a record Belfour set in 2000, and allowed only 6 goals over the last six games.

Turco needed a series like that to cement his status. He needs a lot more, though, to surpass Belfour.

IF YOU COULD'VE BEEN AT ANY GAME IN TEAM HISTORY, WHICH WOULD IT HAVE BEEN?

69 This might be the easiest answer in this entire book: June 19, 1999, the night the Stars won the Stanley Cup. The only quibble might be if you consider it June 20, 1999, the morning the Stars won the Stanley Cup.

Since it was a road game, hardly anyone from Dallas was there. And since it ended so late, plenty of viewers gave up or fell asleep. It was about an hour after midnight in Texas when Brett Hull scored the goal that gave Dallas a 2–1 victory over the Buffalo Sabres and brought the Stars their first championship with a controversial goal scored at 14:51 of triple overtime, ending the second-longest game ever played in the Stanley Cup finals 23 seconds before it became the longest.

Details about the controversy are saved for the next argument. This entry is all about savoring the first major pro sports team title won by a Dallas club not named "Cowboys," and the first Stanley Cup won by a team in the Sun Belt.

While the feat was sealed on this night, it was years in the making.

Start, of course, with Norm Green taking the risk of moving his club from hockey-loving Minnesota to football-loving Dallas in 1993. There was the hiring of Ken Hitchcock, the 1998 signing of Eddie Belfour, and the 1999 signing of Hull, plus the off-season recovery of Joe Nieuwendyk.

This club proved to be something special in the regular season, earning the most points of any team. Their reward was the Presidents' Trophy—not necessarily a good thing, considering only one other winner of that hardware had gone on to win the Cup since the award began in 1985–86.

The Stars opened the playoffs by sweeping Edmonton in four games, but it wasn't as easy as it sounds. The clincher took 3 overtimes. (Foreshadowing?)

There were four overtime games in a six-game series against St. Louis. Then came a thrilling Western Conference finals series against Colorado—seven games, with Dallas fighting out of a 3–2 deficit by winning Game 6 at home and Game 7 on the road.

Buffalo won the Cup opener in Dallas in overtime, 3–2. The Sabres would score only 6 more goals the rest of the series.

OK, back to Game 6.

Jere Lehtinen put the Stars ahead 1–0 midway through the first period. Future Dallas player Stu Barnes tied it with a goal for Buffalo, ending a Sabres scoreless streak that covered 130 minutes, 44 seconds.

There was nothing but tension after that, with each swing of the stick the potential game-winner, a goal that would've won the Cup for the Stars or sent the series back to Dallas for a seventh game.

Dominik Hasek was good in goal for Buffalo that night. Belfour was even better, turning away 53 shots.

A sign in the Stars locker room that night read, "We will either find a way, or make a way." And that's what they did with a lineup featuring five players skating on torn knees, another with a severe groin injury, and Mike Modano playing with a broken wrist.

Between pain-killers and IVs, the Stars did all they could between periods to keep their bodies going. Hull was so out of gas that Hitchcock told him he was done. Then an equipment problem forced Benoit Hogue to the bench and a hard hit, dazed Blake Sloan. That's how Hull wound up back on the ice to score the winning, Cup-clinching goal.

While the Sabres raged about the winning goal, the Stars were delirious with joy.

Team captain Derian Hatcher accepted the Cup from the

commissioner and made sure Modano was the next to touch it. Once Belfour got ahold of it, he became rather intimate with the silver chalice.

In the visitors' dressing room, players shared tears and huge smiles, passing around champagne and giant stogies, many of them celebrating from atop the metal lockers.

So many burdens were lifted.

- Belfour shed his label of not being reliable in the most pressure-packed games by allowing only 9 goals in the finals—none by Miroslav Satan, Buffalo's top goal-scorer all season.
- Hull joined his famous father on the Stanley Cup in heroic fashion, not just by scoring the winning goal but also by overcoming an injury that wasn't revealed until after the game.
- And then there was Modano. The club's top player went from being viewed as merely a goal scorer to a gritty leader, proving his toughness by playing through a broken left wrist suffered in Game 2 of the finals. Despite the pain, he assisted on the Stars' final 5 goals of the series: one in Game 4 and two each in Games 5 and 6. He led the club with 23 points in the playoffs.

The party ended and the team bus rolled away around 4:30 a.m. Their plane landed in Dallas around sunrise on Father's Day, greeted by about 150 people. A few days later, an estimated 115,000 people crammed downtown streets for a parade and 18,000 more packed Reunion Arena for a loud, proud celebration.

I was there for those celebrations. I wish I'd been in Buffalo.

WAS THE STANLEY CUP–WINNING GOAL LEGAL?

70

It counted, didn't it?

The controversial part is that Hull's skate was in the crease. The official explanation on why that didn't violate the no-skate-in-the-crease rule: He had possession of the puck before entering the crease, having kicked a rebound to the blade of his stick.

Folks in upstate New York are still smarting over "No Goal," the cruelest words uttered up there since Bills kicker Scott Norwood went "Wide Right" at the end of Super Bowl XXV. I can handle fans of a losing team holding a grudge. After all, they don't have a trophy to hold. Still, there are some key things to remember about this goal that bring sanity to the debate.

First off, Hull may have violated the letter of the law, but not the spirit. He wasn't camped out there getting in the goalie's way. The same play would not have been questioned the year before or the year after. Heck, just two days later, the league changed the rule, a move that would've happened—but wouldn't have gotten as much attention—had the finals ended any other way. Even more to the point, officials released a statement after the game saying that a March memo circulated throughout the league addressed this exact circumstance, saying it should be ruled a goal. Still, the Cup being decided on such a play had to be their worst nightmare.

Conspiracy theorists thrive in Dallas four decades after JFK was killed here, so it's only fair that a good conspiracy theory is behind this controversy. The idea is something along the lines of the NHL not wanting to call off the victory party after it'd started, like trying to get confetti back into its container after an explosion—not gonna happen.

However, consider what would've happened if the goal had been waved off. Who's to say Dallas doesn't score again anyway to win the game and the series? Even if Buffalo had scored to win Game 6, the Sabres would've then had to come back to Dallas to win a Game 7 against a team and crowd that would've been spitting mad.

The final word on this goes to Lindy Ruff, the Buffalo coach in '99 who was still seeking a Cup when he came to Dallas in January 2007 as coach of the Eastern Conference All-Stars. In an on-ice interview during one of the practices, Ruff was asked about the play.

His answer: "Goal."

WHO HAD THE BETTER TAKE ON HOCKEY: HULL OR HITCH?

71 Ken Hitchcock preaches defense. Brett Hull believes offense trumps everything. Their first year together ended in a Stanley Cup championship. In their second, the Stars returned to the finals. Not a bad mix, eh?

Hull knew what he was getting into when he signed with Dallas in 1999. The team was thought to be a scorer away from winning it all, and he wanted to get his name on the Cup. However, he couldn't think about scoring every second on the ice, not if he wanted to stay on the ice very long.

Hitch didn't turn Hull into a lockdown defender, but he wasn't a liability. Considering Hull's talent, this was likely more of a conscious decision than a coach teaching him how it's done.

Yet Hitch deserves a lot of credit for his role in the transformation of another scorer, a guy named Mike Modano.

Mighty Mo was the top overall pick in the 1988 draft and a 50-goal scorer at age 23. He was labeled a pretty-boy scorer, which isn't always a compliment in hockey circles. It's kind of like the "soft European" label that Dirk Nowitzki wore for so long.

Scoring takes skill. Defense is all about effort—giving up your body and taking on small challenges that don't appear in the stat sheet but earn the admiration of your teammates and coaches. And opponents.

Modano wasn't asked or expected to do those things for much of his hockey life. Everyone else was supposed to dig out loose pucks in the corner, someone else was supposed to check the opposing team's top scorer. Modano was supposed to put the puck in the net.

Then Hitch arrived, took one look at his marquee player and challenged him to be as good without the puck as with it. The result was Modano going all out on both ends, even with a broken wrist during the Stanley Cup finals. He didn't score a goal in the championship series against Buffalo, but he was the leading point man that postseason.

Modano gets most of the credit for transforming himself into a two-way player. Yet Hitchcock gets a hearty pat on the back for having the cojones to challenge his best player like that. The brilliance of the move is that if he could get Modano to buy into it, everyone else had to follow, too.

Even Hull.

DID ANYTHING SHINE BRIGHTER THAN THE STARS FROM 1998–2000?

72

The Stars were easily the best sports-entertainment offering in the area.

The energy in the building was terrific, even though the building was Reunion Arena. By then, fans were knowledgeable about hockey and the stands were a mix of hockey buffs and buff people looking to be seen at the hockey game.

Whether you went to games to see goals or girls, everyone went home happy—usually with the home team winning, especially if good-luck-charm B. J. Thomas sang the national anthem.

The Mavericks had yet to turn games into a full entertainment smorgasbord. While the Rangers were at the tail end of a good run, the Stars still put on a better show, especially in the months when they overlapped.

Think about it: Spend a few hours in the heat watching an early or midseason baseball game? Or go to a Stanley Cup playoff game, where every shift is tense and there's no telling how many overtimes the game might last?

The Stars won the fans over with the right mix of crafty veterans and elite guys still in their prime. Folks could tell this was a special team, so everyone wanted to be in on it. With fans so committed—not just there because it was the place to be, as has happened at the new building—the roars were great, too. The "Dallas! Stars!" chants that punctuated the Pantera theme song never failed to fire everyone up. (Still do.)

I once went to a hockey game at the old Chicago Stadium before it went under and was part of the roar that drowned out the national anthem, the pregame frenzy that set the tone for several hours of mayhem. In Dallas, the roar that punctuated "Stars" in the "Star-Spangled Banner" became a great tone-setter, too, one that still can be heard at times from loyal hockey fans attending Mavericks, Rangers, and Cowboys games. It didn't start during these years, but it certainly was at its loudest then.

To me, the move to the new arena quieted things. I've heard the AAC get real loud, but never as loud as Reunion. Those conference finals against Colorado in 1999 and 2000 might have cracked some decibel meters.

WAS KEN HITCHCOCK RUN OUT OF TOWN TOO SOON?

73

As a Civil War buff who likes to take part in recreations of battles, Hitchcock could probably make a great analogy between his plight and some famous general.

Think about it: Hitchcock worked his way up the ranks, starting by coaching midget leagues in Canada, and then arrived in Dallas in 1995. The Stars were in their third season here and were headed toward missing the playoffs for the first time. If the decline continued, there was a chance hockey in Texas—perhaps even the entire Sun Belt—might fail.

Bob Gainey was a major factor in all this, too. He realized he was better suited to run the front office than the bench, so he removed himself and took the risk of hiring Hitchcock, an NHL outsider. Gainey relied on his experiences winning Cup after Cup with the Montreal Canadiens to find the right balance of skills and personalities for his new coach.

Five straight division titles followed. They had at least 102 points each of those seasons, with the low-water mark coming the year they were playing with a championship hangover; they wound up back in the Stanley Cup finals anyway.

Hitchcock was hard on his troops. Very hard. Too hard, some would say, except that the results showed he knew when to back off.

An unheralded group of veteran leaders—Guy Carbonneau, Mike Keane, Craig Ludwig, and Brian Skrudland—controlled the locker room. Hitchcock was wise enough to let them police each other.

But by 2002, the mood had changed. Players were tired of Hitchcock's style and were tuning him out. A second-round flameout in 2001 was followed by missing the playoffs in 2002. Changes had to be made—and, in hockey, that almost always starts with the coach.

It was the right move at the time, even if the Stars haven't been able to get back to the level he left off. (That's another argument anyway, invoking the question of whether Doug Armstrong is as good of a GM as Bob Gainey was.)

The reality is that hockey isn't like football. Coaches don't last 29 years like Tom Landry—or even four years without any playoff success, like Bill Parcells.

Hitch remains easily the winningest coach in club history, both in total wins (277) and winning percentage (.616). His wit, wisdom, and success guarantee that he'll always be remembered fondly for guiding the club to its first Stanley Cup title.

And that fondess grows with every year that doesn't end in a Stanley Cup.

DOES MIKE MODANO GET ENOUGH CREDIT?

74 This has nothing to do with the Nashville Predators choosing to ignore him scoring his 503rd career goal at their place, even though it made him the leading goal-scorer among all American-born NHL players. This is more about a guy who has been the best player in town for a long, long time, and one of the best in his sport for much of it.

Can you imagine the adulation if a Cowboys player was that good? Consider the explosion of RomoMania in late 2006. By January 2007, there might have been more No. 9 Romo jerseys in circulation than No. 9 Modano jerseys.

Bottom line: This is still hockey; this is still Dallas–Fort Worth.

Within hockey circles, Modano is highly respected. Even casual fans know he's the face of this organization. The ladies certainly know who he is—or, at least, did in his days as Dallas's most eligible bachelor, before he hooked up with one of the women Emmitt Smith beat on his way to the "Dancing with the Stars" crown, model-actress-singer Willa Ford. Crossover appeal is a lot harder. And that's not just for Modano.

Outside of Wayne Gretzky, Mario Lemieux, and new sensation Sidney Crosby, there's not much star power in being great at hockey—especially for someone who doesn't shoot off his mouth or have a famous last name like Brett Hull. (Feel free to bring up my decision to put Dirk Nowitzki over Modano as the latest, greatest local star on my DFW Mount Rushmore, argument No. 2.)

None of this matters to Modano. The game has enriched him and he's made his mark on the history of his sport, regardless of whether anyone in Nashville knows it.

So maybe he's not a widely beloved figure like Emmitt or Troy Aikman, but with a reservation always waiting at his favorite steak house, and a sexy Hollywood star on his arm, Modano has done quite well.

WHAT TEAM IS THE STARS' BIGGEST RIVAL?

75 Edmonton jumps to mind because the Oilers and Stars seem to meet every postseason—or, at least, they did in 1997, '98, '99, 2000, '01, and '03, with Bryan Marchment's cheap shot on Joe Nieuwendyk in '98 adding some fuel to the fire.

But Dallas won every series after '97. That makes the relationship more big brother-little brother, not a rivalry.

So how about Colorado?

The Stars and Avs had some great battles in 1999 and 2000, going the distance in the conference finals both times, plus there were some great verbal jabs between goalies Eddie Belfour and Patrick Roy. High-caliber games between high-caliber teams for high stakes is the perfect formula.

Only one thing is missing: longevity. The teams didn't meet in the postseason again until 2004. Belfour was long gone from Dallas and Roy was retired by then. Colorado won that first-round series in five games, and then did the exact same thing two years later, after the lockout wiped out the '05 campaign. Neither series was memorable enough to rekindle the old flame.

So if the Oilers were Dallas's doormat and the Avalanche were a two-year fling, then who is No. 1 on the hit list? Maybe there isn't one. Or there are just a lot of contenders. So let's switch to the phrase used in the Mavs section: the team you like beating the most. In that case, head to the Motor City.

The Detroit Red Wings have been at or near the top of the Western Conference since the Stars moved to Dallas. From the start, there were several interesting connections between the franchises.

It began with Stars president Jim Lites, who'd spent 11 years as an executive vice president with the Red Wings. He also used to be married to the daughter of the team's owner.

Then there were the coaches: Detroit's Scott Bowman and Bob Gainey of the Stars. Bowman coached the

Montreal Canadiens when Gainey was a star player there.

Bowman brought Detroit the kind of success he had in Montreal, leading the Red Wings to division titles and making them a Western Conference power the years Dallas was trying to get there. Imagine how Michigan natives Mike Modano and Derian Hatcher felt—the team they grew up watching finally got good, at the expense of their own team.

Detroit won the West (and the Stanley Cup) in 1997 and '98, knocking off the Stars in the conference finals in '98. Dallas won the conference the next two years without having to go through them; Colorado spared the Stars the trouble.

This might be a full-blown rivalry by now had those teams met considering how much trouble Dallas had in Detroit even when it was winning everywhere else.

The Stars went 1–3 at the Joe Louis Arena in the '99 and 2000 seasons. The building has continued to be a house of horrors for the Stars, primarily the goaltenders. From Eddie Belfour to Marty Turco to Mike Smith, all can talk about games that seemed like sure wins only to slip away.

Considering how Detroit has been able to sustain success—like winning the Cup again in 2002, having collected Brett Hull from Dallas and Dominik Hasek from Buffalo—the Red Wings should be more of a role model than a rival.

Yet with a good, deep-round playoff series or two, maybe the ties between these teams can spur some spite. Everything else is there.

COLLEGES

WHICH BIG 12 TEAM HAS THE MOST PASSIONATE ALUMS IN DFW?

76 No matter which way I go, this is sure to have folks screaming. Since that's the point of this book anyway, I proudly say:

HOOK 'EM HORNS!!!

Dallas is home to so many large alumni groups and each thinks it is the best. That goes for me and my alma mater.

Drinking from my 2005 national championship coffee mug while writing this, I'll admit us Texas Exes are not always the most loyal. But there's a lot of burnt orange pride going around these days. Mack Brown has the football program going strong, despite the fade late in the 2006 season, and the basketball program is turning into a perennial power. We're always strong in all the other sports, lighting the tower several times a year. And, of course, we've got the best hand gesture and the best cheer.

Quantifying an argument like this ain't easy. You can't just compare membership logs of the alumni groups.

So, using the not-so-scientific method of gauging by

bumper stickers, license plates, license plate covers, T-shirts, hats, jerseys, flags outside of houses on game days, and all other visible means of devotion, I believe Texas, Texas A&M, Texas Tech, and Oklahoma have the largest local followings, followed by Kansas and Nebraska. (Sorry Baylor and Oklahoma State. As often happens on the field, y'all can't keep up with the big state schools in this category either.)

Still, measuring any of this depends on where you hang out. In my surroundings, it's a toss-up between the Longhorns and Aggies, with the Sooners a close third. Then again, anyone who has flown into or out of Love Field on a Friday afternoon, Saturday, or Sunday of a Tech football game in Lubbock knows the number of Red Raiders fans in this area.

The Longhorns and Sooners get an extra boost in this race because of the Texas-OU (*never, ever OU-Texas*) football game.

Until the Aggies and Red Raiders realize the benefits of holding their football game here, Texas and Oklahoma fans will savor their annual excuse to get out in the DFW area and cheer their teams. So what if the local ranks that weekend are swelled by out-of-towners. Seeing all the colors is terrific regardless. It doesn't matter who you root for or against. There's still something special about walking through Fair Park before or after the game, and in seeing that stadium split in half during the game. It's a reminder of how passionate college fans can be.

Another reason to go with Texas in this debate is that

their power base is here: Tom Hicks. Even though DeLoss Dodds calls the shots at the sports department in Austin, he doesn't make a major move without calling the owner of the Stars and Rangers. For instance, Hicks joined Dodds on the recruiting mission that snared Brown.

Oklahoma State can counter with a bigger hitter in Boone Pickens, he of the gazillion-dollar donation or whatever stratospheric number it was. However, it's still Oklahoma State. We can talk about it again when and if that money makes a difference.

WHY IS THE TEXAS-OU GAME STAYING AT THE COTTON BOWL?

77 The Texas-OU game at the Cotton Bowl, in the middle of the State Fair, is without a doubt my favorite sporting event.

Yet it makes no sense whatsoever why the schools have agreed to stay at the old place through 2015 when there's a gorgeous new stadium opening in Arlington in 2009, one so impressive that the Cotton Bowl game is leaving its namesake site behind to play there. (The NFL seems to like it, too, deeming it worthy of hosting a Super Bowl.)

Staying in Fair Park is a much better option than the cash-grab move of turning Texas-OU into a home-and-home series. But, as a Dallas taxpayer, I'm angry that city officials think it's worth pumping money into the old stadium for just a few games a year, even if one of them is this classic.

But this book isn't the place to talk politics. So let's criticize the school politicos instead. The only reason the UT and OU folks agreed to this is because it's what their deep-pocketed alums want. While you have to listen to the folks who pay the bills, the athletic departments should've worked harder to convince the fat cats to move to Arlington.

Think about it: After all the money the schools have pumped into upgrading their own stadiums, they sign a long-term deal to play in an old dump? My guess is that tradition won out, and not just the tradition of the stadium. It's about the experience of going to the State Fair during the day and having lavish parties at night.

Still, it makes no sense.

Consider it from a recruiting standpoint: If you're a teenager, would you rather play at the Cotton Bowl or the fancy new stadium that's home to the Dallas Cowboys? That lure could've benefited both schools.

The pageantry at the Cotton Bowl will still be terrific. But my guess is that they'll realize what a mistake they made and eventually find a way to move this game to a more fitting venue.

Here's my suggestion: Make a deal so that game-day tickets still get folks into the State Fair for free that

Saturday and arrange for shuttle buses to scoot between Arlington and Fair Park, getting everyone to Arlington in time for a late-afternoon game. That way everyone can still get their Fletcher's Corny Dogs and cotton candy and have their nighttime parties.

IS THE COTTON BOWL ON NEW YEAR'S DAY STILL A BIG GAME?

78

Now? No.

Soon? Hopefully.

This may turn out to be one of the best things about the new Cowboys stadium. Sure, having America's Team play there eight times a year will be nice, as will the occasional Super Bowl, Final Four, and other major events it lures.

But with the Cotton Bowl moving to Arlington starting January 1, 2010, there's a chance of getting into the top of the BCS rotation. If so, the glory will return, making this game a marquee event every year, and a whopper of an event every five years or so.

Even if the Cotton Bowl doesn't crack the top tier,

being in this glimmering billion-dollar facility is sure to add some sizzle back to it. Regional lore is great, but a national following—starting with a better TV time slot—is sure to follow.

What often gets lost in any debate that invokes the word *tradition* is that only old people remember it, and college is all about youth. Kids pick colleges for all sorts of reasons, and what happened 30, 40, 50-plus years ago is seldom among them. To an 18-year-old, anything more than two or three years old might as well be ancient history.

That's why the stories about great games from previous eras are nice, but irrelevant. The Southwest Conference is long gone, as is the old bowl system that helped make this game what it was. The powers that be in college sports sent that message when the Cotton Bowl was excluded from the original Bowl Coalition. The early morning time slots given by the television networks is another indication of the nationwide scope of this game—or lack of it.

There was no alternative but to hold on to the "good old days" to try keeping this game on the map. The move to the new stadium should be like the start of a new era.

Sports fans in the Dallas–Fort Worth area should be the biggest winners of this one.

WILL SMU EVER GET OVER THE DEATH PENALTY?

79

The 2007 season marks the 20th anniversary of the year wiped out by the NCAA's first and still only death penalty for rampant violations. The big deal was that boosters were paying players; worse yet, the governor of Texas, a member of the school's board of directors, was in on it. The school chose to scrap another year to make sure the varmints were gone for good. They weeded them out all right. Success apparently was stamped out, too. SMU is no longer a player on the national college sports scene and, sadly, pretty irrelevant locally.

It's a good debate, though, about whether the death penalty is at the root of all the problems.

With it, SMU had no chance of remaining viable in the college sports hierarchy during all the conference shuffling in the 1990s. Baylor needed all the political clout it could muster to hang with the big boys in the Big 12. Plenty of Bears fans wonder whether it was worth it, but that's a whole other argument.

I don't think SMU would've been able to hang in anyway. A small, private school without much going for it in football or basketball would not have drawn the interest from the Big 12 or other power conferences. Instead, SMU wound up in the WAC, then Conference USA—right where it probably belonged.

The lack of success in those leagues is another issue. It seems to me to be more a combination of bad coaching hires and poor recruiting.

Phil Bennett seemed to be the litmus test. He had the credentials to take over a Big 12 program, or to wait for the right one to open up, but instead came to SMU. Many people thought if he couldn't win there, nobody could. He's going into his sixth season without having posted a winning record. The question remains whether he was the wrong guy or if his lack of success proves it can't be done.

Maybe it takes a special player or two. Or the combination of the right player and the right coach—like TCU hit on with LaDainian Tomlinson and Dennis Franchione. Look at the sustained success the Horned Frogs have had since then.

SMU will never be the destination it was for Raymond Berry and Don Meredith, and the lack of payments guarantee future NFL stars like Eric Dickerson and Craig James won't be flocking to campus any time soon. The hope now is just to see the Mustangs become competitive again, able to challenge for their league title, and hold their own in nonconference games against Big 12 schools.

Sizzling college football action beyond Texas-OU and the Cotton Bowl is one of the things lacking in this area. No one expects SMU to change that any time soon, but it sure would be nice if the Mustangs could figure something out.

Just don't hold your breath waiting for it.

WILL TCU EVER BE MORE THAN A BCS SPOILER EVERY ONCE IN A WHILE?

80

Probably not, but the Horned Frogs sure are trying.

Boise State proved in 2006 that going undefeated in a non-BCS conference guarantees nothing, at least not until there's more of a playoff format. Even if there had been one final championship game after the regular round of bowl games, Boise State still may have been left out of the equation.

Second-tier schools will continue fighting for their chance. Hopefully TCU will be among those forcing the issue.

Until then, the folks in Fort Worth need to worry about branding themselves locally. That means getting more Texas teams on their schedule to draw people to Amon Carter Stadium, then showing them a good time.

The Horned Frogs don't have enough of a following in part because of their conference affiliation. Being in the Mountain West means good tests from the likes of BYU and Utah, but it does nothing to excite the locals. Midweek home games and late-night road games only add to the problems.

TCU is in a tough position. So far, the school has done a good job of holding onto coach Gary Patterson and he's done a good job with recruiting to keep it clicking.

The Horned Frogs already have made a couple of runs at crashing the BCS party. Once they break through, we'll see if they—or anyone else—can really shake things up enough to force college football's hierarchy to allow more than the occasional outsider into the ball.

WILL TODD DODGE + NORTH TEXAS = SOUTHLAKE CARROLL'S SUCCESS?

81 First off, Knute Rockne in his prime probably couldn't do for any college program nowadays what Dodge did at Southlake Carroll High School.

Dodge went 19–10 his first two years coaching Carroll, when they were in Class 4A. Then they moved up to play bigger schools—and instantly became the biggest beast in the land, losing only one game in five years and it was a one-point loss in a state finals. That's right: 79–1 and four championships in five years. Wow.

Dodge's powerhouse program drew a call from Bill Parcells when he was coaching the Cowboys to gauge Dodge's interest in joining the staff of the Dallas Cowboys. That never really went anywhere, but a year later North Texas made the bold decision to bring Dodge to Division I-A.

Will it be a brilliant move? Or will it be a reach, like when Notre Dame hired Gerry Faust from a highly successful Cincinnati high school? (Faust won five Ohio titles in his last six years, then went to Notre Dame and never won more than seven games in a season.)

Dodge is in a different situation because of the caliber of his program.

He doesn't inherit as much talent as Faust, who arrived a few years after a national title. Dodge also lacks the Golden Dome and the tradition of the Four Horseman to rely on in recruiting. Plus, much of his success in high school came from an intricate system run by kids who'd been versed in it since middle school. He'll either have to recruit mostly kids from Carroll—like his son, Riley—or he'll have to adapt his system to whatever kids he gets.

Then again, high school seniors were about 12 or 13 the last time Dodge wasn't coaching in the 5A state finals. So his name value goes a long way to the kids he'll be recruiting next fall. There probably will be a carryover effect for a few years, long enough to prop up his reputation until folks can expect some real results with the kids he brings in. Win early and some of his recruiting wars could get real interesting.

North Texas deserves applause for taking this risk.

The Mean Green won't go 79–1 like Carroll did. But Dodge's presence means there's a lot more reason to pay attention to what's happening at Fouts Field.

WHO IS THE BEST PLAYER EVER TO COME FROM A LOCAL COLLEGE?

82 Whoa, Nellie, we're talking about a humdinger of talent from these parts.

OK, enough Keith Jackson schtick. Just trying to set a tone, though, because this is some juicy stuff, football fans.

Here's an interesting tidbit turned up while researching this: Of all Texas schools, SMU is the most-represented in the Pro Football Hall of Fame. The Mustangs have five honorees, tied for the eighth best among all colleges in the nation. Now the trivia challenge—name those five SMU honorees.

Doak Walker and Eric Dickerson are gimmes. I'll save you some trouble by eliminating Don Meredith and Kyle

Rote; great as they were, they're not in Canton.

Still three left. Two were standout players who went on to become head coaches in Super Bowls. The other might be a bit tricky because he never made a tackle or scored a touchdown.

Whether you're giving up or are eager to check your guesses, the answers are: Raymond Berry, Forrest Gregg, and Lamar Hunt.

Sticking with the trivia vein, see if you can name the two TCU products in the Pro Football Hall of Fame and the one from UNT. Just think of North Texas's nickname and you'll think of "Mean" Joe Greene. For TCU, it's Sammy Baugh and Bob Lilly.

Switching to the College Football Hall of Fame, TCU leads the pack with 11 honorees, SMU has 10, and UNT has a pair. Many of these are coaches, including Matty Bell, who worked at TCU and SMU, and Hayden Fry, who went from North Texas to SMU.

Now that we have a bunch of candidates, it's time to begin sorting them out. Let's start by isolating things by era.

TCU's tandem of Sammy Baugh and Davey O'Brien split the 1930s. SMU halfback Doak Walker gets the 1940s. (O'Brien won the fourth Heisman Trophy; Walker won it a decade later, in 1948. No player from a DFW school has won it since.)

It's TCU again for halfback Jim Swink in the 1950s and defensive tackle Bob Lilly, with SMU's Don Meredith sharing some late '50s glory.

The '60s go to UNT's Greene, although special mention goes to SMU receiver Jerry LeVias for breaking the color barrier in the Southwest Conference, with kudos to Fry for making it happen.

Since then, only two players stand out: Dickerson from SMU's "Pony Express" era and the most recent star, TCU's LaDainian Tomlinson.

Almost there, folks.

Baugh and Walker remain icons, with Walker even having an award for the best college running back named for him; O'Brien is similarly honored for the top college quarterback. But since I didn't see any of them, and since football has changed so much, let's respect what they did, when they did it, but leave them out of this discussion.

Lilly's importance already was noted way back in entry No. 17. I'll still give him the nod for top defensive player to come from these parts. Greene gets downgraded for being part of the Pittsburgh Steelers teams that denied the Cowboys two Super Bowls in the 1970s. (Unfair? Tough. My book, my rules.)

Now we're down to two real contenders: Dickerson and Tomlinson. Sorry, L.T. You're well on your way to earning this honorarium. But until you get there, my pick is the high-stepping, goggles-wearing Dickerson.

The standout from Sealy set the NFL's rookie rushing record in 1983, and then set the overall single-season rushing record in 1984. Both records still stand, with the rookie mark (1,808 yards) hardly even getting challenged.

Going into the 2007 season, Dickerson had three of the top 18 single-season totals. Barry Sanders and O. J. Simpson are the only others with multiple seasons on that list, two each.

Dickerson was No. 2 on the career rushing list when he retired and that was without the benefit of playing for great teams. Say what you want about lousy teams having to give him the ball; that also meant defenses knew he was coming.

The bottom line: When Dickerson was good, he was among the best ever.

L.T. may only be a season or two from having the same said about him. He's already the best running back in the NFL and the reigning MVP for the 2006 season, when he broke the record for rushing touchdowns. Having topped 1,600 yards three times in his first six seasons is even more impressive when you look at his receiving numbers. His lowest total of receptions (51) is the same as Dickerson's career high. Tomlinson even caught 100 balls in one of his 1,600-yard rushing years.

If Tomlinson leads the San Diego Chargers to a Super Bowl, this title will be his.

FORE!

WOULD YOU RATHER HAVE A FOUR-DAY PASS TO THE BYRON NELSON CLASSIC OR THE COLONIAL INVITATIONAL?

83 This one depends on your reason for being there.

If it's strictly sights and sounds, the Pavilion at the Nelson tops the plaid jackets at the Colonial. (Actually, the scantily clad women and booze-infused atmosphere of the Pavilion pretty much top everything else on the DFW sports scene when it comes to partying.)

If it's caliber of golfers that draws your attention, the nod again goes to the Nelson—albeit with an asterisk.

When its namesake was personally inviting golfers, presenting them with some handmade woodwork, greeting them at the first tee, and sending them thank-you notes for coming, how could anyone stay away? That includes fans who could've strolled over to the living legend, shaken his hand, and snapped a picture with the only golfer ever to win 11 straight events and 18 in one year.

The 2007 tournament was the first after Nelson's death. Many players surely came to continue honoring Nelson. As time goes on, that pull won't be as strong. Tournament organizers realize that, which is why they are redesigning the TPC Four Seasons course and holding all four rounds there (so long, Cottonwood Valley), starting in 2008, hoping a better layout will help bring back the big names. It remains to be seen how that will work.

If tradition is what you are after, then head out to Fort Worth, make the turn off University Drive across from the zoo and wind through the neighborhood to the Colonial Country Club. With its big white pillars, the main building looks like a country club is supposed to look. The statue of Ben Hogan reminds you this is "Hogan's Alley."

The Colonial has been held every year since 1946, making it the longest running PGA Tour event at one course. Hogan won the inaugural title, of course, and four more. He's still the only back-to-back winner and an upstairs trophy room is a tribute to his great career.

The Colonial is an invitation-only event, and in 2003 an invite went to Annika Sorenstam. It was a PR hole-in-one. And it means she's played in Fort Worth more recently than Tiger Woods. He came early in his career, but hasn't been back, and isn't expected to return any time soon. Still, the Colonial can boast having Phil Mickelson and Sergio

Garcia on its Wall of Champions alongside the first tee, both having won in the 2000s. Previous winners include Arnold Palmer, Jack Nicklaus, Tom Watson, Ben Crenshaw, and Lee Trevino. (Nicklaus, Watson, Crenshaw, Mickleson, and Garcia also have won the Nelson, as have that Woods guy, Vijah Singh, and Ernie Els.)

The marquee names don't always go to the Colonial, but, for pure golf buffs, it's always worth the trip.

If you want to gawk at big names and, uh, other things, hit the Nelson.

Better yet, go to both. Call it research for answering this question if you need to justify it.

WHO WAS BETTER: BEN HOGAN OR BYRON NELSON?

84

It's pretty amazing that two of the greatest golfers of all time were born six months apart, just a few counties away from each other. They caddied together as teenagers, with Nelson beating Hogan by a stroke in a 1926 caddies tournament. Eight decades later, you can still make a strong argument for each as the better golfer.

Hogan is considered among the greatest pure ball-strikers. His book *Five Lessons: The Modern Fundaments of Golf* was released 50 years ago and remains a must-have in every golfer's home.

Nelson's swing was so pure that a robotic swing machine was named for it. "Iron Byron" was used by the U.S. Golf Association to test clubs and balls. The original can now be found at the USGA museum.

Hogan won 63 PGA Tour events, including nine majors, the second most at the time. That includes a career Grand Slam: four U.S. Opens, two Masters, two PGA Championships, and a British Open, winning the only one he played.

Nelson won 52 PGA Tour events, including five majors:

the Masters and PGA Championship twice each, and the U.S. Open once. He was fifth in his only British Open.

Hogan's most memorable year was 1953, when he went 3 for 3 in majors. He missed the PGA because it conflicted with the British Open. He was named player of the year for the fourth time in six years, including the first time the award was given out, in 1948.

Nelson's most memorable year was 1945, when he won 11 straight events and 18 overall, marks that have hardly been challenged.

What Hogan did is even more amazing considering he spent two prime years in the Army during World War II, and six of his majors came after a 1949 car crash that nearly killed him. The wreck—his Cadillac went headfirst into a Greyhound bus—left Hogan with a broken collarbone, pelvis, ankle, and rib. Doctors feared he'd never walk again because of the damage to his left leg.

What Nelson did is even more amazing considering he retired at age 34. He'd already made enough money to buy a ranch, so he gave up the traveling life and settled down. He remained part of the sport by helping groom future major winners Ken Venturi, Tom Watson, and Payne Stewart, and was one of the sport's first TV analysts. He also was the first player to have a tournament named in his honor. He was fortunate enough to witness the Byron Nelson Classic raising more than $94 million for charity.

Hogan was nicknamed "The Hawk" and the "Wee Ice

Mon" (Scottish pronunciation, of course). Nelson was "Lord Byron."

There's no way to pick one over the other. (I'll leave that to you to debate.) So let's change the question to which would you have rather joined for 18 holes?

That is obviously Nelson, as warm and friendly a man as ever walked a golf course, in contrast to the steely, seldom-speaking Hogan.

Nelson was the epitome of a gentleman throughout his 94 years. I attended his memorial service and was awed by the stories of how humble this man was despite all he'd accomplished—in his profession, for his community, and for his beloved church.

A few days before he died, Nelson learned that he was to receive the Congressional Gold Medal, an award that began with George Washington and has been given to fewer than 150 people since.

How do you top that?

WHAT IS THE BEST LOCAL COURSE (High-roller edition)?

85 Anyone who has plugged a tee into North Texas soil knows there are dozens of candidates for this crown. Yet when you scan the "best of" lists that come out each year, three courses are always among the best in Texas: Dallas National, Colonial Country Club in Fort Worth, and Vaquero Club in Westlake.

We'll start with Colonial since it's the oldest—and the only one I've played.

I'm a bit partial to the place since I once won there. OK, it was only the annual Wide Open media event, and I was in a foursome led by the club's top member. Regardless, the tradition and history behind the course, and the quality it maintains, make this country club so unique, so special.

Walk by the Hogan statue on your way to the pro shop. Stand at the first tee and admire the Wall of Champions. Figure out how you're going to attack the fearsome fifth hole, with the Trinity River running along nearly the entire right side, and think about how the pros did it back in the 1941 U.S. Open.

For a duffer like me, Colonial can't be beat. But folks who are serious about their golf also continue to rank this course near the top.

Dallas National is the one with all the buzz, which has been building since before the first turn of its dirt. Of course, a $100,000 initial fee for "founders" of a golf-only facility—no country club, no residential area—tends to get people talking. (So does its No. 59 ranking in *Golf Digest's* 2007-08 list of the country's greatest courses. Colonial, the only other Texas course in the top 100, is 80th.)

Designer Tom Fazio embraced the challenge of building a world-class facility, creating several holes consistently listed among the best in Texas. And if you click over to the course's website, you are greeted by this quote from Fazio: "If Dallas National were the only course I ever designed, I feel I would have had a great career."

Hey, Tom—what about Vaquero, which you also designed?

Here's what he is quoted as saying on that course's website: "I believe that golfers will be amazed by the spectacular beauty and quality of Vaquero. I know I am. Vaquero will be considered one of my most dramatic golf courses."

Perhaps the most dramatic feature is the number of touring pros who have made Vaquero their home course: major winners Justin Leonard, Corey Pavin, and Todd Hamilton, plus Paul Stankowski, Brandt Jobe, Brian Watts, and Ben Crane. Another notable is Hank Haney, Tiger Woods's coach.

Two things that roll call tells you: The golf is good enough to satisfy them, and the amenities make their families happy. That's a heck of a combination.

The winner? How about this: Colonial for one round, Dallas National for several, and Vaquero if you can afford to call it home.

WHAT IS THE BEST LOCAL COURSE (Muni level)?

86 I don't play regularly enough to make an informed selection. But I do know there are plenty of great options available, even for folks who don't rely on connections or deep pockets to play a round. And I know there are so many that at least one is a short drive from wherever you are in the Dallas–Fort Worth area.

Let's start with a pair of true munis, Tenison in Dallas and Pecan Valley in Fort Worth, each featuring a pair of 18-hole loops.

Tenison Glen is Dallas's first city-owned course, dating to 1924. Lee Trevino is among those who learned their way around a golf course by trying to keep balls out of White Rock Creek, which snakes through the course. Tenison Highlands is nicer and newer and costs about $20 more to play.

Pecan Valley offers a River Course and a Hills Course,

with the Trinity River separating them. The River Course is the bigger draw, especially with a $25 green fee on the weekend, among the cheapest on this list.

In Richardson, folks have the option of two Sherrill Park courses, conveniently named No. 1 and No. 2. Farther north in Plano there's Ridgeview Ranch. If you venture even closer to Oklahoma, check out the Trails of Frisco Golf Club. It's among the more expensive in this group, so keep that in mind if you've got a long drive to get there.

Moving back to the heart of Dallas, there's another muni to consider: Cedar Crest, which hosted the 1927 PGA Championship and recently underwent a major renovation by D.A. Weibring's company. Their work, by the way, can be found throughout the Metroplex.

Going west on I-30, you'll find Prairie Lakes Golf Course and Tangle Ridge Golf Club in Grand Prairie. A nice round for a good price also can be found at the Grapevine muni—which proudly has Byron Nelson among its original designers. It, too, has been changed by Weibring's group, with an extra 9 holes added in 1999.

Grapevine also has Bear Creek Golf Club, which offers two courses in a somewhat novel location: the grounds of the DFW Airport. One thing to consider before embarking on a four-hour round there: Make sure you are comfortable with your playing partners. After all, you don't want to be stuck with some jokester who insists on announcing before every drive, "Now preparing for takeoff on the fourth tee box ..."

If you're willing to treat yourself to a luxury round or two, here are some other options to consider.

Start with the TPC Four Seasons, partly for the scenery and partly for the chance to play the course that hosts the Byron Nelson Classic. (Point of pride: I tagged along on a winning team at a media event here, too, so again I'm partial to this place.)

For even higher quality, try The Tribute, in The Colony. Literally a tribute to the courses in Scotland, the game's birthplace, designers took a potentially gimmicky concept and produced 18 terrific holes. The challenge on the links-style course is a unique, memorable experience—so good that it's the state's best public course. According to *Golf Digest*'s 2007–08 list of the nation's greatest public courses, it is No. 78 overall.

The Cowboys Golf Club is another quality layout that also offers a neat experience for football fans. The first NFL-themed course has stone markers referencing historic moments on the gridiron and plenty of memorabilia in the clubhouse. It's all tastefully done, too, without gimmicky tie-ins.

Wherever you go, you've already won. After all, even a bad day at the golf course beats a good day at most other places.

ENDERS

WHO DISAPPOINTED YOU MORE: A-ROD, THE THREE Js, OR BILL PARCELLS?

87 This all comes down to how high your expectations were and how far away the reality turned out to be.

PARCELLS

Did you really expect Bill Parcells to lead the Cowboys to a Super Bowl? Considering the Cowboys' championship pedigree and his, it sure seemed possible.

Parcells came in having been to three of them, plus he got within a game another time. Besides, his specialty was taking losing teams and making them championship material.

But his last title was in 1990. He hadn't reached a Super Bowl without Bill Belichick on his staff. He came out of retirement as much for the paychecks as for the chance to add to his legacy. And he was pretty involved in personnel decisions in Dallas, something he'd never been particularly good at.

Parcells walked away after four years. His tote board: 34–32 with two playoff appearances but without a win either time.

That's definitely below expectations. But not a total failure.

He brought back credibility the Cowboys had lost during the Barry Switzer, Chan Gailey, Dave Campo eras. Simply by taking the job, and keeping it as long as he did, Parcells salvaged Jerry Jones's reputation. The hiring helped Jones's image so much that Arlington voters approved paying for part of his new stadium, something that likely wouldn't have happened had Jones hired another perceived puppet. It remains to be seen how well-stocked Parcells left the roster, but it certainly was better than he found it.

No, he wasn't great. But he wasn't a disaster either.

A-ROD

Did you really expect A-Rod to lead the Rangers to a World Series? Not unless he was going to pitch as well as he hits.

The idea of Texas going from pretender to contender was partly predicated on A-Rod being a magnet, a guy to lure in other star players. It never happened. The best pitcher the Rangers could get was Chan Ho Park, and we argued in the Rangers section about which addition was worse.

Here's how much A-Rod helped: Texas went from 71–91 the season before he arrived in Arlington to 71–91 in his third and final season here. They won 18 more games the year after he left.

THE THREE Js

Here's your disaster.

The Mavericks were terrible in the early 1990s, but after the 1994 draft they seemed to have lucked into something good. In successive years, they drafted Jim Jackson, Jamal Mashburn, and Jason Kidd—a prototypical shooting guard, small forward, and point guard, each taken with the can't-miss expectations that come with being among the top four picks in the draft. Dallas sure seemed to have the makings of a team that could get back to the playoffs and stay there for a long time.

The problem was that the Three Js didn't share that vision. Each saw themselves as more important than the other Two Js. Jealousies, injuries, and other petty problems undermined the whole plan.

Kidd was the biggest star, but was such a pain that he turned out to be the first to go. The others were gone as soon as Don Nelson took over and could find takers for them.

After exorcising everyone from the roster he inherited except Michael Finley, Nellie needed a few more years to build it back up. Finley, Steve Nash, and Dirk Nowitzki turned out to be everything the Three Js were supposed to be. Better late than never.

WHAT'S THE BEST NICKNAME OF ANY DFW ATHLETE?

88 Baseball is usually a breeding ground for quality nicknames. And the Rangers have had some good ones, starting with their first two managers: "The Splendid Splinter" Ted Williams, and Whitey "The White Rat" Herzog.

Jim Kern was "The Amazing Emu" because of his size. Danny Darwin was "The Bonham Bullet" because of his hometown.

Bucky Dent already had "(Bleep)ing" as his middle name when he arrived in Arlington as a player, then a coach.

Others who brought along memorable monikers: Rich "Goose" Gossage, Rusty "Le Grande Orange" Staub, Steve "Bye Bye" Balboni, Dennis "Oil Can" Boyd, Bill "Mad Dog" Madlock, and Burt "Happy" Hooton.

Rick Helling became known as Rick "Shelling," albeit mostly in the media. Hard to imagine anyone ever saying that to the pitcher's face. Another media creation: Oddibe "Young Again" McDowell, one of the more clever nicknames created by ESPN's Chris Berman. (Ridiculous trivia: The first Berman-ism was Frank Tanana "Daquiri," who pitched for Texas from 1982–85.)

Hockey brought us Pat Verbeek—the "Little Ball of Hate" because of his size and pesky playing style. Brett Hull was sometimes referred to as "The Golden Brett," a play off his dad, Bobby, being called "The Golden Jet."

Eddie Belfour was "The Eagle," a common nickname for guys named Eddie. At least Belfour embodied it by having a cool bird painted on his goalie mask.

Basketball hasn't given us much. Remember the failed attempt to get DeSagana Diop as DeSagana "Swat" for his blocked-shot prowess? Another that never caught on: Dirk, Nash, and Finley being known as "Dirty, Nasty, and Filthy."

Nowitzki sometimes answers to "Diggler," a reference to the porn-star character Dirk Diggler in the movie *Boogie Nights*. But you won't hear anyone call him that on national television.

You will hear Avery Johnson called "The General" or "The Little General." It started in his playing days and it's just as apt now that he's the coach.

Jason Terry is known as "JET," but the nickname loses steam when you realize it stands for his initials. (In case you haven't figured it out by now, any play on a person's name doesn't count in this category. No "Boo" for Steve Beuchele, "Newy" for Joe Nieuwendyk, "Stack" for Jerry Stackhouse.)

Others who've passed through the Mavericks: Dennis "The Worm" Rodman, John "Hot Rod" Williams, and Nick "The Quick" Van Exel.

That brings us to the Cowboys.

Ed "Too Tall" Jones, Thomas "Hollywood" Henderson, and Rayfield "The Big Cat" Wright are all top 10 picks. For more recent fans, a big "Mooooose" call for Daryl Johnston, please.

Bob Lilly is, was, and always will be "Mr. Cowboy." The two legendary quarterbacks he played with were "Dandy" Don Meredith and former Naval officer Roger Staubach, aka "Captain Comeback."

Another legend: "Bullet" Bob Hayes.

Cliff Harris was "Captain Crash" for his hard hits. Clint Longley was the "Mad Bomber" for his deep passes and inaccurate ones, though it later summed up his temper.

Nate Newton was "The Kitchen," because he was bigger than a refrigerator—or, rather, The Refrigerator, William Perry. Flozell Adams was dubbed "The Hotel" because he's as big as one and Raghib "Rocket" Ismail sure was fast.

"Triplets" is a classic, and Michael Irvin liked to be called "The Playmaker." He even had it on his license plate: PLY MKR.

Deion Sanders had two nicknames, "Prime Time" and "Neon Deion." Anyone remember his teammate known as "Red Rock"? That was Robert Thomas, a linebacker-turned-fullback.

Kenny Gant was "The Shark," Jason Garrett was "Red Ball," and there were some good rhymes, like "Steady" Eddie Murray and "Swervin'" Curvin Richards.

A great tandem was deep snapper Dale Hellestrae and

Hawaiian Mark Tuinei, who had a radio show called "Snapper and Pineapple."

Some established stars who brought memorable nicknames to their Cowboys days: Lance "Bambi" Alworth, "Iron" Mike Ditka, and a coach known as "The Big Tuna."

Ready for one more? Hope so, because it's my pick as the best this town has seen or heard: "Manster."

Randy White earned that because the way he played he had to be "part-man and part-monster," according to teammate Charlie Waters, who came up with the name.

Clever, apt, and memorable—it's everything a nickname should be.

WHAT'S THE BEST QUOTE EVER GIVEN BY A DFW ATHLETE?

89 Like with nicknames, it turns out the best quips come from the gridiron, with the best of the best involving a guy nicknamed "The Sphinx" because he was such a puzzle.

Duane Thomas was strange, but smart. He uttered one of my favorite sports lines in January 1971, prior to Super Bowl V in Miami. Asked by Frank Luksa if this was the ultimate game, Thomas replied: "If this is the ultimate game, how come they play it every year?" Thomas was a visionary. In a game that gets overhyped more and more every year, he already had it pegged.

Earlier that same season, Thomas spoke out against management at a time when such a thing hardly ever happened. He labeled Tom Landry "a plastic man, no man at all," called Gil Brandt "a liar," and branded Tex Schramm as being "sick, demented and completely dishonest."

Schramm's retort: "That's not bad. He got two out of three right."

Another quotable running back from the same time was Walt Garrison. My favorite from his collection of witticisms came in response to a question about whether Landry ever smiles: "I don't know. I only played there nine years."

Pete Gent, best known for writing *North Dallas Forty,* offered up this zinger during his playing career upon seeing a teammate studying Landry's voluminous playbook: "Don't bother reading it, kid. Everybody gets killed in the end."

Thomas Henderson was a dazzling personality on and off the field. Trying to stir up some excitement for the January 1979 Super Bowl, Hollywood made fun of Steelers quarterback Terry Bradshaw with the memorable line: "He couldn't spell 'cat' if you spotted him the 'c' and the 't.'" Alas, Bradshaw won the game and was named the MVP, which he presumably didn't need the M and the P to figure out how to spell.

Let's close this with a bit of a curveball—fittingly, from baseball.

The trick is that it's not from someone who ever had anything to do with the Texas Rangers. But he is a Dallas native and his line is one of the best in baseball history.

His name: Ernie Banks. His line: "Let's play two!"

WHAT STADIUM/ ARENA IS THE BEST PLACE IN DFW TO ATTEND A GAME?

90 How about the one with the name that just sounds like a great place to spend a few hours: The Ballpark.

That's what I always have called it, and always will. I don't recall ever uttering the phrase "Ameriquest Field"—at least, not in a positive way—during its brief tenure and I don't expect I'll ever use the new name, "Rangers Ballpark in Arlington."

The home of the Texas Rangers will always be The Ballpark in Arlington to me. And I will always remember the goose bumps I got the first time I walked into the place.

Having grown up going to games in The Astrodome, then getting to know Arlington Stadium my first few years here, my threshold for baseball stadiums was pretty low. However, I'd been to games at Camden Yards, Wrigley Field, and Fenway Park, so I knew what a baseball cathedral was supposed to look like. The Rangers nailed it. I thought so then and I still think so—especially when I see the place empty long before or after a game.

A colleague argues that it's a Camden Yards wannabe that isn't. That it's not as good as Minute Maid Park in Houston, and never will be because it's not in a downtown setting. Well, maybe. But it's the best we've got.

For now, that is.

When the new Cowboys stadium opens in 2009, it is going to blow away its neighbor. Jerry Jones is spending about $1 billion on the place—an Arlington tax hike covers the first $325 million, the rest comes from his kids' inheritance—and you can be sure he is going to get his money's worth. The retractable roof will be an area first, and the overhead high-definition monitors inside the place are going to be the biggest in the world.

The Cotton Bowl already has a deal to move there. The Super Bowl is coming in 2011. And don't be surprised if it becomes home to an NCAA men's basketball Final Four, the BCS national championship football game, and maybe an NBA All-Star Game.

Until Jerry World opens, here's how I rank the best of the rest:

1. AMERICAN AIRLINES CENTER

It's a fine place for basketball, hockey, and even the Arena Football League. But it's too corporate and too big to be cozy. Folks who couldn't wait to get out of Reunion Arena kind of miss the quaintness of the old place, though the amenities of the new arena far outweigh the sentimentality.

2. LONE STAR PARK IN GRAND PRAIRIE

Whether you go high-brow and sit in a suite, or spend a few bucks on a general admission ticket, a day at the races is a great experience that can be a profitable one, too.

3. TEXAS MOTOR SPEEDWAY

It's a massive place that can cater to the elite and to those in bare feet. When it opened, so much focus was on gussying up the place that the track itself was neglected a bit.

Eddie Gossage and crew have smoothed out nearly all the kinks, including the traffic problem naturally caused by moving 200,000 people in and out. And they've overcome the political hurdles to get a second NASCAR date.

4. DR PEPPER BALLPARK & LAGRAVE FIELD

From Frisco to Fort Worth, there are two spiffy places to catch minor league baseball.

Dr Pepper Ballpark, home to the Rangers' AA affiliate in Frisco, opened in 2003 as a great alternative for folks in suburbs north of Dallas who hate the long drive to Arlington.

The stadium is big enough and nice enough to have a major league feel, yet the attitude is family-friendly and kids-first, like the minors should be. The all-you-can-eat promotion in 2007 was an interesting lure.

LaGrave Field, home to the independent league Fort Worth Cats, is a new version of a stadium by the same name that was home to minor league teams from the 1920s to the '60s.

The new place opened in 2002 with an emphasis on making fans feel like they've stepped back to the good ol' days. A sign in front lists 46 Hall of Famers who played at the original LaGrave, including Babe Ruth and Hank Aaron. The team also claims to have the only ballpark with four dugouts: the two the teams use, plus the two used in the stadium's first go-round, which can be rented out as suites.

5. TEXAS STADIUM

Like the Cowboys, its best days were long ago.

The most redeeming quality is that it still looks pretty good on TV, especially when they show the championship banners flapping in the breeze through the hole in the roof. Otherwise, there aren't many redeeming qualities.

Jones let the place show its age to help with his escape plan. Now, Irving officials have no reason to spend the money needed to spruce it up. With no tenant on the horizon, it'll be interesting to see what happens once the Cowboys move out.

6. THE SPORTATORIUM

Just kidding. But I wanted to throw a little love to the old, now-demolished place, which is gone but not forgotten by anyone who ever had the guilty pleasure of watching a wrestling match there.

7. PIZZA HUT PARK

Nice place. But not nice enough to justify following driving directions that include the line "go to the end of the North Dallas Tollway, then keep going for a few miles." Plus, they play soccer there.

AAC OR REUNION?

91 Odds are, you've forgotten most things about Reunion, didn't like the place, or maybe even never went there. You may think of it as having been a waste of money considering it was outdated in only 20 years.

Listen up then. You might learn some things that will give you at least a little appreciation for the flat-top building on Sport Street—starting with the fact it was built by a brazen mayor who circumvented voter approval, a clever move considering taxpayers probably would've shot down spending $27 million on a building that had no guaranteed tenants.

Go back to November 1977. Donald Carter and Norm Sonju had never even met, much less started putting together a plan to bring the NBA to Dallas. The NHL wasn't anywhere near the radar. This also was 20-something years before the movie "Field of Dreams" and the line, "If you build it, they will come."

Yet Mayor Robert Folsom knew he had a big-league city. And he got his building through a creative bond plan that didn't require raising taxes, which is why he needed the permission of the city council, not voters.

Critics called it "Folsom's Folly" and "The House That Bobby Built." Putting it next to Union Station begged for jokes about the proposal being "railroaded."

Well, guess what: The very same day the building opened (April 28, 1980), NBA owners voted 20–2 to make the Mavericks the league's 23rd franchise. Dallas became the first team added since 1974, and would remain the only expansion team for eight more years.

As for Reunion, it hosted the 1984 Republican National Convention, the one that nominated President Reagan and Vice President George Bush for re-election. Two years later, Reunion played host to both the Final Four and the NBA All-Star game.

Loud fans proudly known as "Reunion Rowdies" made the place fun during the first great era of Mavericks basketball. The arrival of the Stars brought a much-needed injection of life around the time the Mavs were going downhill.

Things were always lively when the SWC basketball tournament came to town, thanks mostly to Arkansas Razorbacks fans. Cries of "Pig Sooie" are probably still ringing through the rafters. There might even be a broken-down RV or two left in the parking lot.

The indoor soccer Sidekicks also called the place home. There were lots of concerts and tennis matches, plus roller hockey and rugby.

Hockey playoffs during the hot summer months drew lots of complaints about the quality of the ice. Those were trivial compared to all the other complaints about the place.

Reunion's misfortune: It was among the last major sports venues built without luxury boxes, the cash cow that adds glitz and helps pay for the best players. It also was a few thousand seats smaller than many NBA and NHL facilities.

The idea of a new building began as early as 1994. Finally given their say, Dallas voters narrowly approved funding it in January 1998. Reunion was the third-oldest building in the NBA when it was abandoned for the opening of the AAC in 2001.

The new place is gorgeous, first class all the way—like the flat-panel TVs in the elevators.

Bigger isn't always better for an arena because it puts more fans farther from the action. Still, all the benefits of the AAC make Reunion a dinosaur.

The forgotten building with the glassy façade alongside I-35 still holds the occasional sporting event. But there is one plan out there that could make Reunion more popular and more controversial than ever:

Casino.

COTTON BOWL OR TEXAS STADIUM?

92

The Cotton Bowl certainly has a rich past, from Doak Walker to Bo Jackson, Elvis Presley to the Texas Jam, from the turf war between the Cowboys of the NFL and the Texans of the AFL to memorable college football games played there on New Year's Day and those played by Texas and Oklahoma every October.

Alas, it has outlived its usefulness. The funny thing is, so has Texas Stadium, and it is 40 years younger. Both buildings were top-notch in their time, but both of their times have come and gone.

Comparing and contrasting the facilities is meaningless, or will be once the new Cowboys stadium opens. Jerry Jones's jewel will be the equivalent of a top-of-the-line sports car. By comparison, Texas Stadium will look like a rusty motorcycle and the Cotton Bowl could pass for a tricycle with a worn-out seat and a horn that doesn't honk.

Texas Stadium is certainly better, if only because the Cotton Bowl is so decrepit. But instead of getting into the debate of one versus the other, here's a rant against the powers that be in the city of Dallas, two generations of folks who are to blame for all of this.

First of all, the DALLAS Cowboys never should've left the city limits.

City hierarchy could have spruced up the Cotton Bowl in the late 1960s, when it was about as old as Texas Stadium is now. Or they could have had the vision to build a new place. Instead, Irving got the Cowboys and built a stadium that redefined how sports venues were built. While the hole-in-the-roof part didn't catch on, luxury boxes and seat bonds sure did.

About that same time, Dallas politicos also failed to realize the benefits of having Major League Baseball, letting Arlington lure the Washington Senators-turned-Texas Rangers.

At least Robert Folsom was smart enough to get Reunion built.

Had Dallas city leaders played their cards right, Big D could have one heck of a downtown complex with three stadiums for four teams. There would be hotels, restaurants, and all sorts of vibrant activity in the area—daytime, night-time, weekends, etc. Alas, the Sixth Floor museum and whatever remains of the West End are what they have to lure folks downtown. Victory Park may one day enliven the area around the American Airlines Center, but think of how many decades behind the curve it is.

The good news for DFW sports fans is that Arlington had Tom Vandergriff and Robert Cluck, sports-savvy civic leaders who've reshaped our sporting landscape.

And the really good news for folks in Fort Worth is that it's a shorter drive.

ARLINGTON STADIUM OR THE BALLPARK IN ARLINGTON?

93 You had to have been in the old place when the stands were empty to truly appreciate what it was: a minor league ballpark on steroids.

Turnpike Stadium made the leap to a major league facility through pure patchwork. The giveaway was all those outfield seats, more than any other ballpark in the majors; a dubious distinction because those are the lowest revenue-producers.

There was a winding tunnel that connected the home dugout and the home clubhouse. Getting from the press box to the clubhouse after the game required reporters to leave the stadium.

The old Texas-shaped scoreboard was nice while it lasted. The thermometer was depressing. When The Ballpark opened, then-boss Tom Schieffer intentionally left it out. Why remind the customers it was 90 degrees at 9 p.m.?

Arlington Stadium's various expansions took seating

from 10,000-plus in its early days as a minor league stadium to more than 35,000 when the majors arrived. It grew beyond 41,000 with the addition of an upper deck in the late 1970s. The revamping of the outfield scoreboards also changed the wind patterns, turning it into much more of a hitter's park, for better or worse, usually worse.

Many of the best highlights came in its final years, once Nolan Ryan arrived. Some of the other noisiest moments came courtesy of things being banged against those metal bleachers—usually feet, although Bat Night was an annual eardrum-buster.

Turnpike-turned-Arlington Stadium was important in one sense: It brought Major League Baseball to the area. And there were a few other contributions: ballpark nachos, dot races, and the Cotton-Eyed Joe during the 7th-inning stretch. Well, two out of three ain't bad.

The stadium was destroyed in 1994, becoming a parking lot for the new place. Now in its second decade, and on its third name, The Ballpark remains a gem.

One thing architect David Schwarz pointed out on my first visit was the wedge of open air between the Home Run porch and foul territory along the right-field line. That sliver was intentionally left open as a challenge to left-handed hitters, giving them a spot to literally hit the ball out of the ballpark. Decide for yourself which is the bigger surprise:

- Of all the big hitters the Rangers have had, none have managed to do it.

Or...

- Of all the lousy pitchers the Rangers have had, none have served it up.

WHAT'S THE SIGNATURE MOMENT AT TEXAS MOTOR SPEEDWAY?

94 I still find it humorous that the first wreck came on the first turn of the first lap of the first NASCAR race at TMS, courtesy of Darrell Waltrip.

And it was kind of funny that a piano virtuoso played the national anthem before the first race. His arrival via helicopter and performing in a tuxedo were first-class touches, but completely lost on a crowd that was probably more familiar with Mississippi-bred twin brothers Stew and Stan Cliburn, both of whom played major league baseball in the 1980s.

A better feat at TMS came years later, when Dale Earnhardt Jr. won his first Busch and Winston Cup races there. His old man became pretty emotional over the first one; I recall there being a debate over whether tears actually slid under the Intimidator's shades.

The track also has had several races come down to eye-blink finishes. Yet controversy is what seems to, uh, drive this place.

The battle for a second NASCAR race raged from the start, ultimately needing a lawsuit filed by a fan to get it done.

A CART race was canceled hours before it began because drivers were scared of the track. One angry fan was seen holding up a sign that came up with a new twist on the league's initials: Cowards Aren't Racing Today.

The track itself was a source of frustration for years, so much that head honcho Eddie Gossage once wore a T-shirt that read, "Shut Up and Drive." Things quieted after a resurfacing, although more work was done in early 2007 to fix a problem known as "Dale's Dip" because Little E griped about it the most.

All that, though, is merely background for my favorite moment, an episode that combined the best of on- and off-track excitement. Let's call it "The Battle for Victory Lane."

Texas's own A. J. Foyt was there soaking up the adulation for his drivers Billy Boat and Davey Hamilton finishing 1–2 in an IRL race. Arie Luyendyk was third in his first race since winning the Indianapolis 500.

But Luyendyk believed he'd won in Fort Worth, too. He was so sure that he went into victory lane to let everyone know.

Well, A. J. wasn't going to let the Dutchman get away with it. The 62-year-old Foyt smacked Luyendyk twice in the back of his head, then wrapped his hands around Luyendyk's head, took two steps, and shoved him to the ground.

The funniest part? Luyendyk was right.

After an all-night review, the U.S. Auto Club realized it miscounted the number of laps driven by several cars, including Luyendyk's. He actually drove two laps too many!

USAC was fired by the IRL. But you can't get rid of the memory that easily.

DOES ANYONE CARE THAT THERE'S AN MLS TEAM IN FRISCO?

95 I certainly don't.

Spare me the lectures about soccer being the beautiful game and the novella that is every trip up the pitch. Ultimate Frisbee, professional lacrosse, and the beach volleyball tour have a better chance of getting me to buy a ticket. Something interesting might happen at one of those events.

Maybe I was spoiled by the 1994 World Cup because this caliber of soccer does nothing for me. Then again, I'm not alone. Hard-core soccer fans I know would rather watch overseas games in the middle of the night than sit in the best seats on the most beautiful afternoon for an MLS game.

(Important info for fellow soccer spurners: The team formerly known as the Dallas Burn now calls itself FC Dallas. No, the "FC" has nothing to do with them moving to Frisco from the Cotton Bowl. In a ridiculous attempt for European street cred, it stands for "futbol club." Even sillier, the Salt Lake team has the word "Real" in front of its name, but soccer aficionados know that it's pronounced "Ray-all.")

The MLS can import David Beckham and any other past-their-prime overseas players. As long as Americans see the MLS as a proving ground to get a real job elsewhere, then the MLS has got "minor league" written all over it. And in the United States, that's only a good thing in baseball.

Team founder Lamar Hunt was a wonderful man and a brilliant pioneer of sports in the United States. He was among those believing that kids who grow up playing soccer will become adults who support a soccer league.

Ain't gonna happen. Put me among those believing soccer is something American kids run around doing until they're old enough to figure out how to play other sports.

WILL ANY OF THE LOCAL MLS PLAYERS EVER BE MORE POPULAR THAN TATU?

96 No way. The little guy who scored all those goals in indoor soccer games, then threw his shirt into the crowd after every one, was one of a kind. In fact, getting back to the idea of a DFW Mount Rushmore in No. 2, there should be a rest stop honoring Tatu at the highway exit leading to our proposed sports monument.

Tatu dominated the entire indoor soccer world for 20 years. Yes, it was *only* indoor soccer and toward the end the leagues changed so fast that even avid fans had trouble keeping up. But this little guy was such a whirling dervish and so popular that Sidekicks highlights usually made the nightly news. Opponents tolerated his showmanship at their place because they knew it was good for the popularity of their struggling league.

Get this: About 10,000 people showed up for a downtown parade following the team's 1987 MISL championship. Local Baskin-Robbins stores later named a flavor of ice cream in his honor: Tatu Toffee.

Tatu was born Antonio Carlos Pecorari in Brazil. His nickname comes not from the *Fantasy Island* sidekick, but from his dad, who dubbed him the Portuguese word for armadillo.

Tatu averaged more than a goal per game over his career, keeping local jersey-makers busy. He played here from 1984 to 2003, helping the club win four championships. He was a player-coach for his last five years, winning player of the year and coach of the year in 1998, then another title in '01.

It's probably no coincidence that one year after Tatu stopped playing, so did the franchise.

WHAT'S THE BEST LOCAL COLLEGE TEAM IN ANY SPORT?

97

(Hint: The emphasis is on "any.")

This team has won seven national titles since 1991. The latest was in 2006, won in the last second, overcoming the agony of two straight losses in the title game.

Still no clue?

Well, they were honored at the White House in 1993. In 2007, the governor of Texas suggested they get a spot in the *Guinness Book of World Records.*

They are...the UT-Arlington Movin' Mavs wheelchair basketball team.

Upon joining the National Intercollegiate Wheelchair Basketball Conference in 1989, the Movin' Mavs made 10 straight Final Fours. They've produced six MVPs and 16 first-team All-Americans. The program also is the first and only one that has every member on a full athletic scholarship.

Top that TCU, SMU, or UNT!

Another local branch of the UT system is dominating its sport. Well, "sport" might be a strong word. Competition is more like it. The team is the UT-Dallas chess squad, and it is already recognized as a national powerhouse among pocket-protector wearers.

UTD followed its victory in a prestigious December 2006 event by winning the 2007 Final Four of Chess. They didn't lose a single match, winning it all by the widest margin in the seven-year history of the tournament. While that might not mean much, this should: Duke finished fourth.

UTD has won three of the seven Final Fours. The school—which competes in Division III baseball, basketball, soccer, softball, volleyball, cross-country, golf, and tennis—actually has a six-figure budget for chess. It's a clever PR move, linking UTD with brainiac success. But, hey, for our purposes, a collegiate title is a collegiate title.

WHAT WAS THE BEST SPORTS MOVIE FILMED IN THE DFW AREA?

98 Philly has *Rocky*. We had scenes of *Invincible*, the story about Vince Papale making the Philadelphia Eagles out of a tryout camp, filmed at Texas Stadium.

Notre Dame has *Rudy*. We had *Necessary Roughness* filmed at North Texas. This one might not be all that lopsided, though, especially if you are anti-*Rudy*. Our cheesy film did feature Kathy Ireland, credible actors Hector Elizondo, Scott Bakula, and Jason Bateman, plus comedian Sinbad.

The Rookie was filmed in Arlington, and it's a decent flick, especially since it's a true story about a Texan who really did make his big-league debut in Arlington. Other liberties are taken in the film but, hey, that's Hollywood.

Any Given Sunday is another movie filmed at Texas Stadium. It was only a so-so movie considering the impressive collection of talent: Al Pacino, Cameron Diaz, Dennis Quaid, Dallas-area native Jamie Foxx, James Woods, Matthew Modine, Ann-Margaret, all directed by Oliver Stone. (Here's a nugget for you: The title of that film can be traced to a novel of the same name written by former

Cowboys defensive lineman Pat Toomay. It even got him a bit part in the movie as an opposing coach.)

The nod here goes to another book penned by a former Cowboys player. If you haven't already guessed, it's *North Dallas Forty*, the thinly veiled novel—and screenplay—written by ex-receiver Pete Gent.

Anyone familiar with it and the local sports of that era can easily crack the code: The Cowboys were the "North Dallas Bulls," Nick Nolte was the celluloid version of Gent, Mac Davis plays the quarterback reminiscent of Don Meredith, and the coach obviously is modeled after Tom Landry. Whether the religious, good-boy backup quarterback is supposed to be Roger Staubach remains a point of conjecture. But there's no doubt about the real-life inspiration for offensive lineman Stallings: former Cowboys lineman Jim Boeke, who played the role.

Consistently ranked among the best sports movies of all time, *North Dallas Forty* was a different spin on sports than Hollywood usually produces starting with some of the harsh realities of the game.

In addition to the emphasis on the daily aches and pains, there's this classic eruption from O.W. Shaddock, played by former Oakland intimidator John Matuszak: "Every time I call it a game, you say it's a business. Every time I say it's a business, you call it a game!"

The movie did a nice job of blending satire, drama, and sex with sports. No wonder the NFL brass hated it.

WHICH TEAM'S RADIO CREW IS WORTH HEARING WHILE WATCHING A GAME ON TV?

99 The genesis for this concept comes from football. Too often the national broadcasters don't know the teams well enough, or they talk about the other side too much. Since true fans want to hear the game slanted through the eyes of the Cowboys, the club has always provided top-notch talent to make it worth the effort.

For most of the last 30 years, Brad Sham and his partners have been so good that folks at home weren't the only ones tuning in. Thousands of fans bring radios to Texas Stadium to hear what the crew is saying. In turn, Sham often caters to them, saying things like "for those of you at the stadium who aren't seeing this replay" or pointing out things for fans inside the stadium to see.

There were a few unfortunate years when Sham wasn't in the booth. And 2006 wasn't a must-listen with Charlie Waters as the analyst. Things should be back to normal with Babe Laufenberg returning in 2007.

The hockey tandem of Ralph Strangis and Daryl "Razor" Reaugh are wonderfully entertaining, too, even when the Stars aren't. They've also been great teachers of the game to an audience that needed to be taught a lot about hockey.

Of course, they're immune to the radio-TV volume thing. Their broadcasts already go over both airwaves.

As the Mavs have improved in recent years, so has the quality of their radio shows. Mark Followill was so good he got promoted to TV. That paved the way for Chuck Cooperstein's knowledge and passion on radio. Different styles, both are a great listen.

The Rangers have seldom been as good as the quality of their broadcasters.

Mark Holtz was among the best ever, with his signature line of "Hello, win column!" a welcome treat from 1982 to May 1997. He was forced out of the booth by leukemia, which took his life a few months later. His memory lives on after every Rangers home win, when his trademark phrase is flashed on the center field scoreboard. Holtz, by the way, moved to the DFW area to be the first voice of the Mavericks. The basketball team honors his memory with a college scholarship endowed in Holtz's name.

The years Holtz and Eric Nadel were paired together, the quality of their broadcasts usually exceeded the quality of what they were describing. Holtz actually left for the TV booth in 1995, with Sham taking his place.

Nadel has since worked with Vince Cotroneo and Victor Rojas, keeping the radio broadcasts worth listening to—even if it's just to hear his latest rendition of "A Page from Baseball's Past."

So, the real winner in this category is us listeners.

WHAT'S ON YOUR CAR RADIO: THE TICKET OR ESPN RADIO?

100 Since this book was billed in the introduction as being "sports talk in book form," this is the perfect place to finish.

The answer to this final item probably depends on your slant on sports. Or your mood at the moment. Maybe even which hosts are on at the time. Or which teams.

If you like sports mixed with a bunch of other things guys talk about, then 1310 AM, The Ticket, is the place for you.

If not, flip over to 103.3 FM, ESPN.

The ratings show The Ticket has more P-1s than ESPN. In fact, "P-1" (loyal listeners) is among the many words and phrases that have seeped into the local sports vernacular thanks to the folks at The Ticket, from the gentle musings of Dunham and Miller in the morning, mid-days with Norm

Hitzges, then BaD radio (which I never listen to), and The Hardline in the afternoons. Since 2006, the Ticket—and its FM sister stations—also carry Dallas Cowboys games.

ESPN programs are more rooted in sports: The national perspective during Mike & Mike in the Mornings and The Dan Patrick Show in early afternoon; the local view during the mid-morning Little Ball of Hate Show and late-afternoon Galloway & Company. Regardless of the show, there are frequent visits by folks who work for other ESPN properties. As self-serving as it seems, the cross-promotion usually works because those folks are either insightful, entertaining, or both. ESPN also carries Mavericks games.

As for picking a final winner, I'll call this one a tie. See, I don't care which station you pick—or which newspaper, website, TV station, magazine, etc. I just hope you are following the Dallas–Fort Worth sports scene closely enough to have opinions on players, teams, and issues, and that you're willing to debate about it all.

That might be the one thing everyone reading this book can agree on.

INDEX

A

B

C

D

E

F

G

H

I

M

N

O

P

S

T

Y

Z

ABOUT THE AUTHOR

Jaime Aron has been covering sports in Texas for The Associated Press since 1991, and has been the Texas Sports Editor for AP since 1999.

Along the way, he's covered five Olympics, three NBA Finals, two Stanley Cup finals, a Super Bowl, a World Series, a Final Four, the Breeder's Cup, and the Pan Am Games. He received the state Sports Story of the year award from The Headliner's Foundation in 1999 and was named the national AP Sports Writer of the Year for 2001.

He also is the author of *Tales from the Dallas Mavericks* and coauthor of *I Remember Tom Landry*.

Jaime lives in Dallas with his wife, Lori, and their sons, Zac, Jake, and Josh. The Arons proudly served as the Ambassador Family for the local chapter of the March of Dimes in 2007, helping raise money and awareness in the fight against prematurity in hopes that more families can have the happy ending they've had. For details, visit www.jakeandjosh.net.